SNIPPETS
Little Bits of Life
Captured and Shared

Sometimes, life happens in big chunks but more often, it's those small pieces or SNIPPETS of everyday events that bring us laughter, smiles and special memories for years to come.

"...have a little laugh at life and look around you for happiness, instead of sadness..."
Red Skelton

"Life is what happens to you while you're busy making other plans."
Allen Saunders

By Ann Lovvorn Douglass
© 2017

Contents

CAN I HAVE THAT BABY?

Now most four-year old children have no idea where babies come from nor whom they belong to. They just magically appear in those tiny little plastic beds all lined up in that white room behind the glass window at the hospital – or so I thought.

With my fourth birthday just around the corner, I was about to be admitted to the Marietta Hospital on Cherokee Street to have my tonsils out. I didn't really know what tonsils were. All I knew was that I had been sick a lot and Mamma and Daddy told me having my tonsils out would make me feel better. They also said I could have all the ice cream I wanted. Sounded good to me.

The hospital was all white and smelled funny. The hard marble floors made a lot of noise when we walked on them. Nurses all wore stiff white uniforms with little white hats and white shoes. Everything was

5

white. I didn't really like white that much. It would have been much prettier if it had been pink.

The next day I woke up in a metal bed in that white room. My throat hurt really bad! I cried and that made my throat hurt more. Daddy offered me some water but I didn't want any. Then he offered me ice cream but I just cried. Nobody told me that my throat was going to hurt when I had my tonsils out! Finally, Daddy asked me if I would like to go to the nursery and see the tiny babies. I liked babies a lot and said yes.

We walked down a long hall until we came to a room that was filled with tiny babies in tiny plastic beds. The door to the room had a window on the top half and the window was open. Daddy picked me up so I could see all the babies. I liked that.

I asked Daddy if I could have one of the babies and he said yes, if they didn't belong to anybody else. He told me to pick out the one I wanted. That was hard to do. I liked them all. Finally, I picked out one that was wrapped in a pink blanket. Daddy asked the nurse to bring that one to the window. The baby was so little but I knew I could take good care of her. Daddy asked the nurse if that baby belonged to anyone. She smiled and said yes that it belonged to someone else. Daddy said that was okay that I could just pick out another one.

I spent a long time choosing another baby. The next one had a blue blanket. The nurse brought him to the window but said that one belonged to someone else also. I was disappointed but I picked out another baby. The nurse brought her to the window but then she said that one also belonged to someone else. We stayed at the nursery for a long time and I picked out so many babies that I wanted but everyone I picked out belonged to someone else. Finally, I was tired and thought some ice cream might taste pretty good. The next day I went home from the hospital – without my tiny baby.

TURNIP GREENS AND CATSUP

"...but I really don't like turnip greens!" How many five-year-old little girls do you know who like turnip greens? From my vantage point as one of those five-year-old girls, I was sure NONE of them did. They didn't even look like something you would eat. It was like trying to eat slimy green leaves that had fallen off the trees in the back yard. There was nothing fresh or crisp about them. Even celery would have been better than that! At least celery was crisp and a pretty shade of green. It was even crunchy when you bit into it. But when you put the yukky turnip greens in your mouth, the only thing you could hear was your tongue screaming, "Get that outta here!"

However, my opinion was of no consequence to my mother when she prepared the evening meals. At least once a week, the slithering, slimy greens appeared on our supper table. Now, it would have been fine if I could have just turned my head and pretended they were not there – but no, it was worse than that! Not only was I not allowed to ignore them, I was expected to EAT THEM. Granted I was only five, but after all, doesn't it say somewhere in our U.S. Constitution that kids have rights too?

I protested, I pouted, I cried – why I even begged and pleaded, but all to no avail. There on my cute little plastic plate sat that blob of green. Perhaps Mamma wouldn't notice if I just moved the stuff around and tried to hide it under the other food on my plate. Didn't work. "Ann, eat your turnip greens!" Why I would have even given up dessert if I could have avoided the fate of the greens. Obviously, it didn't matter if I ate dessert or not, I was not allowed down from the table until those greens had vanished from my plate.

Then, Daddy came to my rescue. He didn't like turnip greens either but he was taller than I was so he didn't have to eat them. There was something very unfair about that. Anyway, he knew I loved catsup so he suggested we just cover the greens with catsup. I agreed to try, hoping I didn't succumb to food poisoning! Well, it really wasn't so bad. I put a small bite in my mouth, held my breath, closed my eyes really tight and swallowed. Down it went. Fortunately, it stayed down. Spitting it out was not an option at our dinner table. But that's another story for another time. So, as the years passed and I grew into adulthood, I continued to eat catsup on turnip greens whenever I was required to consume them.

One New Year's Day many years later, my husband Duane had cooked the traditional dinner of black-eyed peas and (yep, you guessed it) turnip greens. We packed the delicious delicacies and drove over to his mother's house to share our meal with her.

By that stage of my life, I was so accustomed to eating catsup on my greens that I didn't realize most people would think it quite bizarre. As I covered the greens with the beautiful red catsup, my sweet mother-in-law looked a little puzzled and inquired what I was doing. I told her it was a long story but I had eaten them that way most of my life. Well, she decided to try it. And would you believe, she loved it and to this day, she won't eat turnip greens without catsup!

5TH GRADE REPORT CARD

From the day, I entered the hallowed halls of Blackwell Elementary School as a brand new first grader, I LOVED school! That is, until several years later when I received my 5th grade report card. Learning always came easy to me, requiring very little effort. All my report cards up until that time exhibited only "A's" – not even one "B" had disgraced my school record.

However, all that changed when my fifth-grade teacher distributed report cards for the first six weeks of school. To my horror, I opened my report card and what did I see??? It was a "C" right there in front of me. Quickly, I closed the report card, fearing someone would detect my fall from grace.

That afternoon as I slowly got off the school bus and began walking the short distance to my house, my stomach was one big knot! Mamma always asked to see our report cards as soon as she got home from work and since my mother happened to have been Valedictorian when she graduated from high school, she expected no less from us three children. Time was of the essence. I had about an hour to devise a plan to correct this dreadful twist of fate.

I finally figured it out! Reaching in my notebook, I retrieved my freshly sharpened number 2 pencil. I would simply correct what must have been a horrific oversight by my teacher. I was sure she intended for me to have all "A's "on my report card as I always had. Very carefully, I placed my pencil on top of the "C" and made an "A" out of it. There, problem solved! No one would ever know...

When Mamma and Daddy arrived home from work, they immediately asked to see our report cards. My older sister, Louise proudly showed off her exemplary all "A" report card and my younger brother, Arthur cheerfully held his out for viewing. When asked where mine was, I tried procrastinating but that got me nowhere. Finally, I quickly slid it on the edge of the dining room table hoping they would simply glance at it and sign their name. However, that didn't happen.

Mamma picked up the report card, looked closely and held it up to the light. Then she showed it to Daddy. Daddy looked at me and asked if there was anything I would like to tell them. "Nope", I replied, "Everything's fine." The grueling continued. Mamma again inquired if there wasn't something I'd like to tell them. "Nope, not a thing." Then they suggested that Louise and Arthur might like to go outside to play. Finally, I could breathe. As I rushed toward the door to join my sister and brother, Mamma said, "Not you, Ann. We need to talk." Oh dear, I knew I was dead!

My secret was out. They were sure "someone" had altered my report card so I decided to explain. Being completely confident that I had done nothing wrong, I began by telling them that my teacher was sort of old and had probably just made an innocent mistake. I was only helping her by making the "C" into an "A". Then I asked them what made them notice. They explained that the teacher had written all grades in blue ink and I had written over it in number 2 pencil. Oh, I hadn't thought about that. Anyway, feeling sure they would appreciate my helpfulness, I asked if I could go out to play.

Certainly not, I was not going out to play! They were calling the school and they would go with me the next morning to the principal's office! Surely, they weren't serious! But indeed, they were. Early the next morning, I walked into the principal's office, flanked by Mamma on one side and Daddy on the other. Mr. Henry Hill, the principal, asked us to be seated. Then he turned to me and said, "Ann, I believe you have something to tell me", to which I responded, "No, not really."

After being prompted a second time, I confessed that I had helped my teacher because she made a terrible mistake. "Is that right?" he asked. Well, he said we needed to get it straightened out so we would all just go down the hall to my fifth-grade class and chat with my teacher.

Oh no, he couldn't be serious! I told him that wouldn't be necessary that I had corrected her mistake and I was not angry with her. He insisted so I led the way followed by the entourage of parents and principal. We walked in the room and students filled every desk. Surely, this discussion would not take place in front of the whole class – but it did.

Mr. Hill asked me to tell my teacher what had happened. And so, I began… "…you see, I know you didn't mean to but you made a terrible mistake on my report card. I am not angry or upset with you and I have corrected your mistake so I'll just take my seat and Mamma, Daddy and Mr. Hill can leave. As I walked toward my desk, the teacher, in a rather loud voice instructed me to return to her desk. Well, to make a long story short, let's just say I never again attempted to "help" any of my teachers with their grading system. If they made mistakes, they just had to live with them!

UNMENTIONABLES

In our rural country life, such luxuries as clothes dryers were unheard of. Although we did have a washing machine, clothes were hung on the clothes line outside to dry. My sister Louise and I were responsible for doing the laundry during the summer months. Normally, that would not pose a problem. However, one sunny afternoon one of the neighborhood boys came to visit when I was hanging the clothes out to dry.

Now I was too young (about 12 or 13) to think about these boys as anything other than "boys." We had all grown up together, had picnics together, ridden bicycles together and even shot BB guns together. However, they were a few years older than me and for some reason, Daddy thought that was a bit of concern. It was many years later before I understood his thinking.

Well, as I was reaching into the laundry basket to pick up my "unmentionables" to hang on the line, one of these "older" boys rode up on his bicycle. Quickly, I dropped the unmentionables back in the basket and picked up a dishcloth instead, hoping he'd just wave and keep on going. But, no he didn't. He stopped right beside me and the laundry basket and asked me what I was doing. It was obvious what I was doing but politely I told him I was hanging out the clothes to dry. "Oh," he replied and just kept standing there.

I was being very selective about which items I chose from the laundry basket to hang on the line. Towels, sheets, shirts, socks, etc. were all fine. He was watching very carefully as I clipped the items on the clothes line with the wooden clothes pins. Finally, all that was left were my "unmentionables".

Now I might clarify that I did not own any frilly or lacy unmentionables. Most of our unmentionables were made by Mamma out of good sturdy muslin fabric. Never had any lace since that would have been a wasted extravagance. No one was supposed to see one's unmentionables anyway. I guess she never anticipated that one of the neighborhood boys might come for the viewing on laundry day.

Well, it was a terrible dilemma for me. I could either be brave and go ahead and expose all my unmentionables for the boy to see or simply leave them in the basket and hope they would dry by themselves. I decided Mamma would be mad if I didn't hang them out to dry, so I tried very inconspicuously to pick up two pair at once and hang them together, just so I could get done quicker.

16

Just as I was about to clip the wooden clothes pin securing them to the cloth line, I dropped them. They fell <u>right at his feet!</u> Horrible dilemma for me! Should I reach down to get them or just crawl in the ground?

Being the young gentleman, he'd been taught to be, he reached down and picked them up and handed them to me. I thought I would die right then and there. He had touched my unmentionables!!!!!! Oh no, I could never show my face in public again. Swallowing hard and being as nonchalant as possible, I simply reached for them, threw them back in the laundry basket and told him I had things to do inside. He inquired if I was going to finish hanging out the clothes (Bet he just wanted another "viewing"). I said no, that I would finish later – maybe at midnight when nobody was around.

SUNDAY SCHOOL TEACHER

From the time I was a young child, I loved to play school and I was always the teacher. That love carried forth into Sunday School at Roselane Baptist Church in Marietta, GA. I always went to Sunday School each Sunday and enjoyed it a lot. However, there was one Sunday School class that never could keep a teacher. It was the 9-12-year old's. For some reason, the students in that class didn't behave very well and whenever they got a new teacher, the teacher would only stay a couple of weeks, then would leave.

I decided that was the perfect opportunity for me to teach. I was thirteen at the time and felt fully qualified to teach. So, one Sunday after church, I approached the Sunday School Superintendent (who was about a hundred years old) and informed him I would like to be the teacher for that class.

He patted me on the head and asked how old I was. I replied that I was old enough – that I was thirteen. He

18

smiled and said maybe someday when I was older, I could teach. I assured him I was old enough and that I knew I could do a good job! Again, he patted me on the head and said he was sorry but I was too young. (Why is it that very old people like to pat very young people on the head?) Anyway, I asked him how old a person had to be to teach and he just mumbled something about being a grown-up. I was determined so I finally asked him who was going to teach that class if I didn't do it. He didn't have an answer and he finally said I could do it.

Well, long story short – I absolutely LOVED teaching that Sunday School class! Although I was only a year older than most of the students, we had a great time – maybe it was <u>because</u> I was only a year older... Anyway, the small group of 10 students quickly became 20, then 30, then 40 students. We put on pageants and plays for church services, we had ice cream socials, we took trips together. We even studied the Bible together. What a great group of kids!

I don't know that I was really qualified to be a spiritual leader to the students but suffice to say, we all learned and grew together. God has a way of guiding and taking care of His children.

Interesting tidbit: Many years later, I was attending a high school alumni function. A middle-aged woman walked over to me and said, "Ann, you probably don't remember me but you were my Sunday School teacher at Roselane Church." Yes, I certainly did remember her! She was a dear sweet person who had graduated one year after I did from Sprayberry High School...

AWKWARD SITUATION

As teenagers, our social hub was the young people's group at our church. We had a large group of young people and enjoyed many social activities together. In fact, church was probably more of a social activity than a spiritual one. There were lots of girlfriends and boyfriends and going to church regularly gave us extra "date times". After all, what parent would say no when asked if we could go to church every Sunday morning, Sunday night and Wednesday night prayer meeting?

At the Sunday morning worship service, there were two choir lofts – a regular adult choir and a young people's choir. Both were at the front of the sanctuary. The adult choir was to the left of the pulpit and the young people's choir was to the right of the pulpit. Both were usually filled to capacity.

One Sunday morning, I was sitting next to Fred in the young people's choir. Fred was a sophomore at GA

Tech and I was a sophomore in high school. He had asked me to go out on a date with him but I had declined. Although we were supposed to be singing, he was secretly whispering to me. Then it was time for the morning offering and Fred was one of the ushers who was going to pass the offering plate. He got up from his seat in the choir, stepped down to the congregational rows and proceeded to pass the offering plate.

Meanwhile, another good friend named Buddy walked into church. He was three years older than me. He was getting ready to join the U.S. Air Force. He had also asked me to go out with him but Daddy said I was too young.

Buddy was a bit late arriving for church services and as he walked in the entrance which was at the back of the sanctuary, he scanned the room for a seat. Seeing the empty space next to me in the choir, he walked directly to the front of the church, up into the choir loft and sat down beside me. The young people in our choir began snickering. One of the boys sitting behind us reached over, patted Buddy on the shoulder and whispered, "Way to go." I felt my face flaming but Buddy had no idea what had just happened. He leaned over and asked me what the boy meant by his comment. I just shrugged my shoulders and said we should be quiet.

Meanwhile, Fred was still passing the collection plate but was looking very angrily at me and at Buddy. By then, the whole congregation was snickering. Fred finished with the offering collection and looked up to the choir. There was no place for him to sit. I suppose I should have told Buddy that the seat was taken when he first came up to sit down but this was all playing out right in the front of the church – and it was a small church. I mean, the preacher was sitting just a few feet away. I thought maybe they could both squeeze back in the space when Fred finished ushering. Probably that would have worked if I had sat in one of their laps. I just couldn't decide which lap I wanted to sit in. Fred finally chose a seat in the congregation and the service continued. It's probably best not to share the conversations which took place after the final Amen...

"FUN" IN THE WATER?

Growing up in the South, many summer days were spent enjoying the swimming pool or vacationing at the lake. As a child, I always found the water exhilarating. Soon I noticed that my friends had all learned to swim as had my sister and brother. But, for some reason, that was a skill I never mastered. I tried everything. I even put "floaties" in my swim suit. Believe me, I was MORTIFIED when they floated out. Everything floated, but me!

As the years passed, I enrolled in more swimming classes than I can remember but it was all to no avail. I paid attention in class and tried everything I was told to do, but I concluded I must have been made of lead for inevitably I sank like a rock.

When I was a teenager, we spent a lot of time at Allatoona Lake with our friends. My boyfriend Fred's parents had just bought a place at the lake. One Sunday after church, Fred took me to the lake to see his parent's property. Their lot was a pie-shaped lot with a wide swath of beach area on the lake. We walked around the property then decided to go down to the beach area at the lake. Being the svelte young teenager, I thought I was, I headed down toward the lake at a swift run. Oops! I didn't see the strings that had been staked out where their cabin was ultimately going to be built. Down I went – head first. Although I was not hurt, my pride was permanently damaged (I thought). What a wonderful first impression I made on my future in-laws!

Fred owned a beautiful mahogany inboard motor boat and he loved to water ski. In fact, he and most of our friends had been skiing since they were young children. I was slightly behind times but I wanted to impress him by learning to ski with grace and ease.

Fred said he would teach me. Down to the water we went, carrying two wooden water skis. First, I made sure my life jacket was fastened securely, then into the water I went. Fred was driving the boat and yelling instructions to me.

As I was bobbing around in the water with what felt like twenty pounds of lumber attached to each foot, I tried and tried. Each time the boat tried to pull me out of the water, I fell and came gasping up for air. Fred's patience (or lack thereof) was wearing quite thin and being yelled at really didn't help me at all! All this was a bit frightening since I didn't know how to swim but I continued to try over and over. My arms ached and I felt as though I had swallowed half of the water in the lake.

Finally, I had an epiphany! If I couldn't learn to ski on two skis, then I'd learn to ski on just one! I told Fred to give me the slalom ski. He protested vehemently saying I had to learn to ski on two skis first. I insisted and finally he agreed, all the while assuring me I would not be able to do it. But, I did!

Success at last! The first time the rope went tight, up I came. I skied around the lake and never fell once. I couldn't swim and I couldn't ski on two skis, but I quickly learned that I could ski quite well on a slalom ski. I was proud of myself!

Fast forward a few years…
When I was in Graduate School, I was completing my Early Childhood Practicum in an affluent pre-school environment. One of our requirements was to take the little three and four-year olds to the local swimming pool. I was quite embarrassed when I had to tell my supervisor that I couldn't swim. She was very gracious and said I could just stay in the shallow end of the pool with one of the little boys who was afraid of the water.

Each day for a week, we went to the pool. His golden hair formed ringlets framing his face as he splashed in the shallow end of the pool. I began teaching him all the things I had learned in my (unsuccessful) swimming lessons. He was delighted. By the fourth day, he was swimming and loving it.

At the end of the week, his mother came up to me with tears in her eyes. She was so appreciative that I had helped her son loose his fear of water and learn to swim. I thanked her, thinking, "if she only knew...

GRANDMA'S FRONT PORCH

Spending Saturday afternoons at Grandma's house was a ritual my sister Louise, cousin Jeanne and I frequently enjoyed during our childhood and early teenage years. We were actively engaged in chatter, giggles and discovering "boys".

Those leisurely afternoons with Grandma rocking in her rocking chair on the front porch were instrumental in forming our innocent impressions of what "proper young girls" should and should not do. Grandma felt it was her responsibility to guide us in the mores of the times (late 1950's).

First was proper dress for respectable young ladies. All young girls over the age of ten must wear girdles to church every Sunday. When we walked we must never let anything wiggle or shake. Although I never understood what there was on a slender little 95-pound female body that could possible wiggle or shake, apparently Grandma thought something could.

28

White gloves were a must for Sunday dress. Whenever seated, proper young girls must always be sure their dresses covered their knees.   Additionally, shorts were NEVER to be worn on Sundays nor was it proper to have a date on Sunday.

Although Grandma was married, she didn't seem to espouse any joys from matrimony. Many times, she would turn toward us three young girls sitting on the metal glider on the porch and say, "Lordy, you young girls – I feel so sorry for you just knowing what you have ahead of you!" Now, we never knew exactly what she was referring to but we decided it must have something to do with boys.

 She frequently admonished that once we were grown and married, that we must always rise early before our husbands, dress and brush our hair, put on our nicest apron and have hot biscuits awaiting hubby when he arose. We would laugh and reply that we wouldn't do that, that we would make our husbands get up early and cook biscuits for us! You would have thought we had cut off her right arm as she replied, "Oh Lordy, don't you girls ever let anyone hear you say that!" Those were indeed the "Ozzie and Harriet" days.

Grandma, as might be assumed, spent the biggest part of her days in the kitchen. She rose early and prepared a huge breakfast which usually consisted of bacon, ham, eggs (cooked to order), grits, homemade jam and naturally, delicious hot biscuits. Her dining room table was large enough to easily seat twelve people. It was always covered with a white lace tablecloth. The table settings were complete and properly arranged. To sit down at her breakfast table and say, "I think I'll just have a piece of toast this morning" would have been a cardinal sin!

After everyone finished breakfast, she cleared the table, washed and dried the dishes. Then it was time to start preparations for lunch. Lunch would consist of at least one or two meat entrees plus a variety of fresh vegetables. (I don't think the word, "sandwich" was in her vocabulary.) After lunch, it was cleanup time again. Finally, after all the dishes were put away, she had about two hours before time to start supper. In the South, we called the evening meal, supper. That short rest time was enjoyed watching her favorite soap opera on television, *As the World Turns*.

Every morning Grandma read the local newspaper and the first section she read was the Obituaries. Then she would announce that she had to go down to Mayes Ward or Dobbins Funeral Home later that day because Bessie Smith or Lula May Hopkins or some other unknown person to us had died. When asked who that person was, more than likely she'd reply that she had no idea but it was important to go pay her respects anyway. Paying one's respects was a very important part of our upbringing. And although Grandma did "have her ways" we always loved and respected her.

MY FIRST JOB

It was a big move to reach the status of sub-freshman (8th grade) as I officially entered high school. Along with high school status came the desire for more stylish clothes. I had learned to sew at a very early age, consequently most of my clothes I made myself. It was many years later before I fully appreciated that skill.

Realizing "store-bought" clothes cost money and my allowance was a meager $1.25 per week, I decided I needed a job. Now, I didn't want just ANY job, I wanted to choose my job and I wanted something I would enjoy! I was not interested in working in the 5 & 10 cent store nor did I want to wait tables in the local restaurants.

On a cool autumn afternoon when my family made our weekly trip to Marietta, I decided that was the day I was going to find my job. I wanted to look at all my options before making a decision so I walked around the town square twice, carefully looking at each business establishment.   I went inside a few businesses and tried to visualize myself working there. Finally, my decision was made! I decided I wanted to work at Loudermilk Photographic Studio.

I walked into the Studio, introduced myself and announced to the owner, Mr. Horace Loudermilk that I had chosen his place of employment for my first job. (Little did I know that Mr. Loudermilk knew all my family and had done photographic work for them for many years.) He smiled and asked me how old I was. I told him I was thirteen. Then he wanted to know if my parents knew I was looking for a job. I told him no but assured him they wouldn't mind. My disappointment was huge when he told me he didn't have any job openings at the time but he might call me later. I had fully expected to go to work that day!

Before I returned to meet my parents, Mr. Loudermilk had already telephoned my daddy and asked if he knew I was asking about a job. Daddy said no, he didn't know but he wasn't surprised. Fortunately, Daddy thought it was amusing. He was not upset nor angry.

A couple of months later, Mr. Loudermilk called and asked if I still wanted a job. I was thrilled! He said I could work every afternoon after school and on Saturdays. He would pay me $30 a week. That was a lot of money for a thirteen-year-old in the late fifties. Then he asked me how I would get from school to work each day. It was only about five miles. I assured him that would not be a problem that I would either walk or hitch-hike. He didn't think either option was a very good idea so he told me he would give me a book of taxi tickets with my paycheck each week. I was to make arrangements with the Victory Cab Company to pick me up after school every day and take me to work.

My job was everything I hoped it would be and more. I loved it! At first, I just kept the studio neat and tidy, then Mr. Loudermilk began teaching me how to use the camera and how to develop film. The more I learned, the more I loved it.

Within a few years, Mr. Loudermilk's vision began deteriorating and he began asking me to do more and more of the photographic appointments. One day, an older gentleman came in to have his photograph taken. He had been a friend of Mr. Loudermilk's for many years. Mr. Loudermilk went through the motions of the photo session, then he asked his friend if he minded if I also did a photo session. Mr. Loudermilk explained that he was "teaching" me. The friend patted me on the hand and said he always believed in young people learning a trade so that was fine for me to practice. Mr. Loudermilk thanked him and assured him that he would only receive the "professional" prints. Well, little beknown to the older gentleman, he did receive the "professional" prints but they were taken by me, not Mr. Loudermilk!

Mr. Loudermilk was a dear, dear person and I enjoyed every minute that I worked in the studio. I continued my employment until I graduated from high school. The last few years, we never shared our little secret with the customers. As his vision continued to deteriorate, Mr. Loudermilk always went through the motions of the photo sessions and I was always the young apprentice. Customers always thought they were receiving "professional" prints taken by Mr. Loudermilk when they were actually getting the photographs I had taken. Mr. Loudermilk's dignity was preserved and I was happy to play a small part in that preservation.

COLLEGE CAREER BEGINS

Right after high school graduation, most of my friends headed off to college. They were eagerly anticipating college life, dorm rooms, independence, and new friends. I chose a different direction. I got married two weeks after my high school graduation. Thirteen months later, we were the proud parents of our first daughter, Angela. Two and a half years later, we welcomed our young son, Robert into the world.

Now, I had always planned to go to college, but it was getting to be a little more challenging with two babies in my life. However, my belief was, "never say never." A few months after my twenty-second birthday, I decided it was time. I was going to begin my college career!

Early on that cold, rainy January morning I packed the diaper bag and headed out with my eleven-month-old son, Robert and three-and-a-half-year-old daughter,

Angela. I had no transportation since my husband drove our only car to work so I asked a friend to drive me to the local college to register.

It was a very long day spent waiting in very long lines. With one baby perched on my hip and the other tugging at my skirt tail, I had been so naïve.
Quite erroneously, I had assumed I would just run in and register. Little did I realize, it would take EIGHT LONG HOURS! However, I did it! I was beginning my long-awaited college career at about the same time most of my peers were completing theirs.

Seven years later and after the arrival of Allison, baby number three, I graduated! Listening to the strains of Pomp and Circumstance, I proudly stood in my cap and gown with the gold tassel draped around my neck. Joining several hundred other graduates, I graduated Cum Laude receiving a Bachelor of Science Degree in Early Childhood Education with a minor in French.

My dream of teaching unfolded immediately after graduating. Dr. Henry Hill offered me a job at Kincaid Elementary School in Cobb County, Georgia. Yep, that was the same Henry Hill who had marched me down to my 5th grade teacher to "discuss" my altered report card. I guess he saw some redemptive qualities in me after all. The new school was on the cutting edge of everything new in education. I was thrilled!

I loved teaching but I decided it was important to continue my education and began graduate studies. With two years of teaching under my belt, I enrolled in graduate school. I taught school each day and attended graduate school four evenings a week. Eighteen months later, I received my Master's Degree in Special Education.

After twenty years in the classroom, my promotion to Administration brought about a new twist in my professional life. Excited as I was, it meant I must enroll in a post-graduate program to attain my Specialist Degree in Educational Administration. Yep, you guessed it – I was the oldest student in the class! However, I didn't really feel very old, I was only fifty.

I decided a new hairstyle might be in order. Perhaps, "touching up" the color just a bit might also add youthfulness. So, I surveyed the hair product aisle at the local Wal Mart and chose a nice shade of ash blond and a very curly permanent. After a long day of curling and coloring, I was pleased with the results. I'd never worn my hair in the very curly style but it wasn't bad and the color was perfect – at least until the roots started showing. Twelve months and many long hours of study later, I was awarded my Specialist Degree in Educational Administration.

INTERLOBAL LABOTOMY

The day began just like any other day. My three children and I scurried around in the morning getting ready for school. My two oldest, Angela and Robert caught the school bus to their local high school and the youngest, Allison headed out to middle school. I arrived at Kincaid Elementary School where I was teaching at the time.

Now, it might be worth mentioning that this was in the era before cell phones. I know that is very difficult for the younger generation to comprehend, but it's true. There was really a time in history that telephones were actually attached to the wall with cords and they sat on tables or desks. The only thing we held in our hands was the receiver into which we spoke while having a (short) conversation.

Now, back to the incident at hand. I was busily teaching a room full of third graders when an announcement came over the loud speaker. There was an important telephone call for me from my son's school. Oh dear, was he sick? Had he been in an accident? He was fine that morning. Quickly, someone was sent to my classroom to stay with my students while I rushed to the front office. Since my classroom was in a trailer out on the back forty, I had quite a trek. I was out of breath by the time I reached the front office and the school secretary handed me the telephone receiver. The office was full of teachers and students. All eyes were on me.

"Yes, this is Robert's mother." It was the attendance clerk from the high school. In her very soft, consoling voice, she inquired how Robert was doing following his surgery. Surgery? What surgery!!! My head was spinning. That boy had definitely NOT had surgery! Trying to gather my thoughts, before I could respond, the sweet little attendance clerk said, "I received your note (I had not written any note!) but exactly what is an INTERLOBAL LOBOTOMY? Is it some kind of dental procedure?" Then she expressed concern and condolences about the WEEK of school Robert had missed and how hopeful she was that he would be able to return soon. I assured her he would be returning the following day and that he would be making up ALL the assignments he had missed.

INTERLOBAL LOBOTOMY??? What kind of child had I raised? Certainly, I had always encouraged creativity in my children but that was too much! Meanwhile, everyone in the front office was continuing to stare as I tried desperately to regain my composure. The school secretary asked if everything was alright and I assured her everything WOULD be alright very soon.

Finally, taking a deep breath, I thanked the school secretary for calling me to the telephone and returned to my students.

Now, as I said, there were no cell phones at that time so Robert had a few hours' reprieve until I got home that afternoon. I was at home waiting for him when he cheerfully walked in the door (at the same time he normally would have gotten home if he HAD been at school).

"Hi, Mom. You're home early today." "Well, yes I am. I was a little worried about you." Suddenly, wrinkles appear across Robert's teenage brow as he inquired why I was worried about him. When I asked how he was feeling, he quickly assured me he was just fine. "Are you sure?" I inquired. Beads of perspiration began to appear on the teenage brow. Well, I continued, recovering from an INTERLOBAL LOBOTOMY takes a long time and the attendance clerk at your high school said everyone was very concerned about you. OK, now he knows he's been busted! Trying to maintain my composure and the volume of my voice, I asked my dear sweet teenage son what in the world he thought he was doing? Perhaps it's best not to relay the remainder of that conversation. Just suffice it to say, Robert fully recovered from the "surgery" and fortunately has never had a relapse!

ROOKIE PRINCIPAL

My own office, my own desk and computer! What more could I want? I was a newly appointed Principal at one of the local elementary schools and was feeling very confident.

Oops! Was that a fire alarm? My well-trained staff and students immediately evacuated the building in a nice orderly fashion. Then the sirens came blaring as multiple fire trucks and police cars descended on the campus. Firemen in full regalia came running into the school, looking for smoke and fire. Police were stationed on the main road to the school redirecting traffic.

Was that a television satellite being set up outside the building? YES! The local news station was broadcasting live about the horrible fire at the local elementary school. But, where was the fire??? No smoke, no blaze, no nothing!

What we did have was a precious little olive- skin, brown- eyed, curly- haired kindergartener who wanted to know what that red handle was on the wall. And yes, he did indeed find out. Well, maybe I wasn't so confident after all...

As principal of one of the oldest schools in the county, I was privileged to inherit all the roaming ROACH BUGS who made their residence there. Now, I am not a prima donna, but I am not real fond of the creepy crawlers!

At the beginning of the school year and at regular intervals throughout, each teacher was issued a case of Roach Motels as we lovingly called them. These were to be placed strategically in their classrooms to discourage the roaches from bonding with the students.

One day in mid-December, I was engaged in a difficult parent conference in my office. The parent was not happy about anything. As I tried my best to assuage her frustration, I glanced at the wall behind her and to my horror, a large roach bug was slowly crawling toward her. What was I supposed to do? Did I dare confess to the unhappy parent that we were plagued with certain unwanted creatures at the school and ask her to move or should I try to ignore it and pray that it did not fall in her hair? I finally decided to offer her a cup of coffee which allowed me to step between her and the wall and inconspicuously brush the culprit off the wall. Fortunately, my foot was close enough to where it fell that I silently sent the little critter to his heavenly home. Tragedy averted for that moment.

As I so often did, I decided to capture a bit of the humorous situation through verse. Oh, the life of a ROOKIE PRINCIPAL...

Muses of a Rookie Principal
By Ann Lovvorn Douglass

It's almost Christmas and I don't feel so well
Indeed, many stories I do have to tell
In my very first year as a principal I'm told
This job can make one grow wrinkled and old

Teachers out sick or the One Day Sale
To fill the vacancies, the Sub-Finder failed
The lunchroom's rocking' with girls and boys
While the monitor eats cookies, and plays with toys

The roach bugs rampant on holiday fare
Is that a nit in little Johnny's hair?
The clinic monitor again out for the day
Sick children in the office on the chairs do lay

Construction paper needed of red and green
The warehouse reports our order not seen
So, you see, 'tis a sad plight to tell
It's almost Christmas and I don't feel so well.

$15.00 CHRISTMAS

Fortunately, I was blessed with a mother who knew the value of a dollar. From a very early age, we were taught to save our money and not spent it frivolously. Each Saturday when we received our $1.25 allowances, Mamma took us to the bank and we deposited one dollar into our savings accounts. We were allowed to keep the remainder.

Many years later, when I was struggling financially as a single mother of three, that training was a life-safer. I was working full time as a teacher and going to graduate school four evenings a week. With Christmas fast approaching, I was trying to save every penny that I could.

One day I had been visiting Mamma and she asked how I was doing. Of course, I knew what she really meant but being very independent, I simply replied that I was doing fine (NOT). She asked if I needed anything and I said no. Then she handed me a twenty-dollar bill. I refused and assured her that I was fine and didn't need anything. She insisted, saying I could just keep it for emergencies. Unbeknown to me, she slipped it into my jacket pocket as I was leaving. When I got home, I found the money in my pocket and cried. That twenty dollars enabled me to buy groceries that week.

During that period of my life, there were no frills. Having clipped coupons, shopped sales and saved diligently for several months, I finally had a total of $15 to spend on Christmas for my three children - $5 each.

Scouring thrift stores and garage sales, I succeeded in buying a few small trinkets for each. The children never complained. They seemed to have a second sense that for that year, that was the best we could do and that was OK. In fact, my son, Robert had won a 25-pound bag of laundry detergent at his workplace holiday party and he gave it to me for my Christmas gift. Wow! That was wonderful! I never knew laundry detergent could be so uplifting.

SMEGLET

Once upon a time, I had a surreal experience with a little guy named Smeglet. Now Smeglet was first introduced to me as a sweet little pet owned by my 18-year-old son's good friend, John.

But first, a little history about John and how he came to live with us. The summer after my son, Robert graduated from high school, he came home from work one evening and as we sat down to dinner, said, "Mom, I need to ask you something." Sure, no problem. Well, he proceeded to tell me that he had a friend named John who didn't have anywhere to live. John had also just graduated from high school and it seemed he was homeless. Robert asked if John could come live with us. Now, that posed a bit of a dilemma. I had never met John and didn't know anything about him but Robert assured me he was a very nice young man.

I told Robert that I would need to meet John first, then we could discuss his living arrangements. The following night John came to our house for dinner. John was a rather large young man, probably about 350 pounds. He was wearing a very faded red sweat suit that lacked a few inches meeting in the middle. His hair was a bit scruffy and it looked like it had been a while since he had had the opportunity to shave. I was a bit taken aback but decided to give him the benefit of the doubt.

Although John was obviously nervous having dinner with our family, he was very polite and always responded with, "Yes ma'am or no ma'am."
The following day, Robert asked me what I thought and could John come live with us. I told him I would need to speak to John's father first. John's father assured me it was fine for John to live with us. So, I said okay. The next afternoon, John came home with Robert. All of John's worldly possessions were tucked away in a brown paper grocery bag and he was still wearing the very faded red sweat suit.

Our house only had four bedrooms and each bedroom was occupied so the only option was to put a mattress on the floor in the foyer for John's makeshift room. He was very appreciative and never complained. We all learned to step over, under and around whatever was on the floor.

A couple of months later, one night at dinner, Robert and John said they had a proposition for us. Our house had a full, unfinished basement and the boys decided they could finish the basement and make a nice apartment for them to live in. They said they had priced all the materials they would need and it would only cost $500. They assured my husband and I that they would do all the work if we would pay for the materials

Of course, we were pretty sure the construction project would cost well over $500 (and ultimately it did – about ten times that amount), but we decided it would be a good learning experience for the boys. So, construction began. The boys worked every evening after they got home from their jobs and little by little they began collecting thrift store furnishings to complete the project. Long story short, after a few months, they apartment was "livable" and they both moved to the basement. At last, we could move the mattress out of our foyer.

One afternoon I went downstairs to the basement apartment and noticed a strange little animal on the kitchen counter. Inquiring as to the nature of the little critter, Robert said it was John's pet, that it was a gerbil. The gerbil's name was Smeglet. Although my children had had gerbils as pets when they were young, this little critter didn't look much like a gerbil. It had a very long tail and was quite a bit larger than a gerbil but Robert insisted that the man at the pet store where they got it said it was a gerbil. (And of course, all 18 and 19-year-old boys always tell their mothers the truth – the whole truth and nothing but the truth!) Anyway, I tried to be positive so I just told Robert that

John could keep it but he had to keep it in a cage. So, John agreed and Smeglet moved into his "gerbil cage."

Well, Smeglet was a healthy little guy and soon he had outgrown his cage. John had to stack books on top of the cage so Smeglet wouldn't escape. But escape he did – around 3AM in the quiet of the night.

As I lay sound asleep in my bedroom, I was suddenly awakened by something that scurried across my face. I woke up with a scream, startling my husband into near heart-failure! When he asked what was wrong, I told him something had scurried across my face. Very patronizingly, he assured me that I had just had a bad dream and that I should go back to sleep. So, I laid back down and tried to sleep. Just as I was dozing, once again something ran across my head. My blood curdling scream terrified my husband. My voice had reached the level of hysteria as I yelled for him to turn on the light and find whatever monster was in our bedroom!

With the lights illuminating the room, hubby began searching all around the bed and furniture. I sat in the middle of the bed holding my knees pulled tightly against my chest. Finally, hubby said, "I found it." It was Smeglet and he was behind our large triple dresser. He pulled the dresser out from the wall and tried to catch the long-tailed creature. All to no avail, Smeglet could outrun the fastest sprinter. Hubby got the broom and tried to swat him out – no success.

Finally, I gingerly climbed off the bed and went downstairs to the basement apartment and banged on the door VERY LOUDLY! Robert and John finally came to the door half asleep. I told John he needed to come get Smeglet right then or Smeglet would not be around to welcome another sunrise. John apologized profusely and immediately came upstairs to the bedroom. He peeked behind the dresser where Smeglet was hiding in the corner. Then, John stooped down, held out his hand and whispered in a very soft voice, "Come on, Smeglet. Come on over here." And would you believe, Smeglet slowly crawled right into John's hand!

As it turned out, Smeglet wasn't really a gerbil. He was a full-fledged RAT! AND I DON'T LIKE RATS OF ANY SHAPE OR SIZE!!! So, it was best that Smeglet find another home – and he did.

John and Robert continued to live in their little basement apartment for another year or so, then decided it was time to head south to Florida State University. Both boys had been accepted at FSU and a new world awaited them. Fast forward a few more years. Both boys ultimately graduated from college and earned graduate degrees. Both are successful in their careers and have wonderful families. And John has a new wardrobe. Gone is the faded red sweat suit and about 150 extra pounds. He grew into a very handsome young man. Maybe a mattress on the floor of our foyer really wasn't so bad after all.

IS SOMETHING BURNING?

Being a grandmother is absolutely one of the best things ever. I love it! But, sometimes, in my excitement, I guess my brain disengages.

When my oldest, daughter, Angela was preparing for the birth of her precious daughter, Alyssa, she had meticulously organized every detail for big brother, Seth's care while she was in the hospital. She had a schedule of babysitting duties for me and Ruth, the other grandmother. Of course, Grandmother Ruth and I were both thrilled to take care of Seth. He was delightful!

On the day Angela and new baby daughter, Alyssa were to come home from the hospital, my husband and I drove to our daughter's house early that morning. I spent most of the morning playing with two-year-old Seth and his toys. I decided to cook a pot roast for the family to have for dinner that night. I put the roast in the oven, did a little housework and continued playing with Seth. I suppose we were having too much fun because I forgot about the roast.

Suddenly, I smelled something burning. After racing to the kitchen, I spied the charred hunk of meat which was meant to be a delicious dinner. At about the same time the smoke alarm went off. Not wanting the shrill alarm to frighten Seth, I quickly ran into the kitchen, removed the smoking pan from the stove, threw it outside. I climbed up on a kitchen chair and fanned the blaring alarm with a dish cloth. The house quickly filled with smoke. I opened all the windows and fanned the smoke with dish towels to try to get it out of the house. All the time, I was reassuring Seth that nothing was wrong. (Even at the tender age of two, I'm sure he realized that his beautiful home was not normally filled with gray smoke.)

About that time, Grandmother Ruth called to say she was on her way over to their house. Now, Ruth was always meticulous about cleanliness. She even cleaned the baseboards in her house so I surely didn't want her coming into a house filled with smoke and burned pot roast on my watch.

I searched in vain for some air freshener to eliminate the smoke. I found some apples in the fridge which I decided would work just fine as an air freshener. Quickly I cut up the apples, added some cinnamon, put them on the stove to cook and hid the burned roasting pan. Ruth arrived a few minutes later and the first words out of her mouth were, "Ann, I smell something burning!" Oh well, I tried to cover my faux pas.

Later that day when the happy parents arrived home with Seth's new little sister, the house was reasonably okay. Unfortunately, they didn't have the roast for dinner as I'd planned. But, as I said, sometimes in the excitement of a new grandchild, it's not uncommon for a grandmotherly brain to completely dislodge and disengage from the body.

THE THREE QUILTS

The pink patchwork butterfly quilt lay folded neatly on the top shelf of the linen closet. Nestled close by was the orange, blue and yellow appliquéd butterfly quilt. Absent from the shelf was the rustic quilt with appliqued brown suede horses. I designed and made each of these quilts for my three children. My oldest daughter, Angela received the quilt with the large pink butterfly. The quilt with the orange, blue and yellow appliquéd butterflies was for Allison, my youngest daughter. My son, Robert, the middle child requested a quilt with horses on it.

When my children were young, each of their quilts was the centerpiece of their room. The walls, carpet and accessories were all coordinated to match their special quilts. The daughters' quilts were treated with care and they survived the years with minimal wear and tear. After each of the girls was grown and left home to begin their independent life, their quilts, much like their favorite dolls and stuffed animals were left behind. My son, on the other hand always had his quilt on his bed, thrown over a chair or snuggled in the floor. When he left home to go off to college, his quilt went with him.

One day when Angela's daughter, Alyssa was about eight years old, she spent the day with me. We loved doing sewing projects together. She brought her collection of nine American Girl Dolls and announced that she wanted to make nine pair of overalls so each doll could have a pair to wear. That turned out to be a really fun project. By evening when her dad came to pick her up to go home, we had completed all nine pairs.

While Alyssa was at the house that day, I thought she might like to see her mother's quilt so I carefully got it down from the top shelf of the linen closet and spread it out on the bed. She ran her small hands across the large patchwork butterfly. She asked if she could sleep under the quilt that night. For several months, every time she spent the night with us, she slept under her mother's quilt. Finally, one day, she asked if she could take the quilt home with her and put it on her bed. So, off the pink butterfly quilt went to reunite with mother and child.

Not long thereafter, Allison's seven-year old daughter, Ashley was visiting. I had taught her to sew and one of the first things she made was a quilt for her doll. I mentioned the quilt I had made many years earlier for her mother. Carefully I took the blue, orange and yellow appliqued butterfly quilt from the top shelf in the linen closet and spread it over the bed. Her small hands outlined the butterflies as I explained that the very room we were in was once her mother's bedroom when she was a child. Soon the blue, orange and yellow quilt was sent to be reunited with mother and child.

My son, Robert's quilt never made it to the top shelf of the linen closet. Where ever he went, his quilt went with him. The suede appliquéd horses began to wear a little thin and many of the hand-stitched threads loosened. The years passed and as he got older, so did his beloved quilt.

One day as he returned home from work, his young wife was cleaning out some closets in their new house. She had a pile of things destined for charitable donations or for the nearest trash receptacle. She asked him if he would deliver them. Underneath the large pile of clutter, he spotted his ragged quilt. After quickly recovering it, he inquired why it was there. His wife, not knowing the history replied that it was just an old, ragged quilt that she saw no need in keeping. The faded, worn quilt was quickly retrieved and saved from its ill fate.

With the passage of time, the quilts live on. From daughters to granddaughters, the butterfly quilts are now tucked away in new hearts and homes. Robert's quilt may still be lying around or it may have made that dreaded journey into oblivion. Either way, I'm confident it also still lives on in the heart of my son. You see, quilts are more than fabric and thread. They create warmth for today and memories for tomorrow. They are the patchwork of the heart carefully sewn together with love and patience.

PESTILENCE AND PLAGUE

During Biblical times and throughout history, many people have experienced pestilence and plagues. However, I never imagined I would experience such catastrophes!

For several months, we had had a water problem in the basement of our home. Now I don't mean a small water problem where a little trickle of rain water would seep in under the door. I mean a HUGE problem. If Noah had been around, he would have been glad he built the Ark to avoid drowning in our flooded basement.

Fortunately, I had purchased a top-of-the-line wet/dry vacuum. Whenever it began raining, the first thing I did was rush to the basement and assess the flooding. That usually meant dragging out the wet/dry vacuum and suctioning up thirty to forty gallons of water from the floor, then setting up several box window fans to dry out the floors and walls. Had we just had an empty concrete block basement, it wouldn't have been so bad. But we didn't. We had a finished 2200 sq. ft. apartment and my sister, Louise lived there. Believe me, she was not happy when the floods came.

In an attempt to correct the problem, my husband hired a contractor who (supposedly) specialized in water problems. He convinced us if he dug up the sidewalk outside the house, replaced some water pipes and put in a French drain on the outside of the house, our problem would be solved. Well, about $800 dollars and two months later, we held our breath when the next heavy rain came. Guess what? I was back in the basement wrestling the wet/dry vacuum trying to keep from drowning.

As if the problems with the flooding basement were not enough, we discovered we had **MICE** in the basement. They were nibbling away on the food in Louise's pantry. She wasn't very happy about that either. Hubby hired an exterminator who was supposed to be very reputable. Unfortunately, he was one of the good ole' boys but not a very good exterminator. His solution was simply to put cages and rat poisoning all over the basement. That didn't work either. The mice just multiplied. So, by then, we were dealing with flooding AND mice.

I am normally a very calm person and not afraid to tackle difficult situations but this was getting the best of me. I was sure I was on my way to a full-fledged nervous breakdown. Then, when going downstairs one day to check on the status of the mice, I noticed a mound of granular substance that looked like sawdust on the floor at the foot of the stairway below the ceiling rafters. Lo and behold, we had termites!!!

I called the termite exterminator who came out the following day. He insisted we had major termite damage and said the front porch of our house needed to be torn down. So, our lovely home took on the appearance of a construction zone! The exterminator then drilled holes all over our basement walls. It was an awful mess! The exterminator was terrible to work with. Every time he came, he acted like it was a social call rather than a business call. He came inside and chit-chatted about all his past life experiences. I assume he was a very lonely man, but he needed to find other outlets for his waning social life!

Life was getting pretty stressful at our house. Tempers were short and frustration was high. Between the floods, the mice, and the termites, I was ready to sell what was left of our modest little home and move to a tent. I decided I had to take another approach to solve these problems. I had been too nice to all the supposedly reputable contractors.

I started by researching how to correct flooding, mice and termites. Then, I fired the exterminator and hired a reputable exterminating company. Within a few weeks, all the mice and termites were gone. Under the guidance of a skilled contractor, our front porch was rebuilt. To stop the basement from flooding, I hired another company. They came out to assess the situation and fore-warned me that I wouldn't like what they had to say. However, they were honest and told me the only way to correct the problem permanently was to dig a trench around the perimeter of the <u>interior</u> walls of the basement, then install a French drain and a sump pump inside the basement. It was a very noisy and messy job with jack hammers drilling through the concrete floor and concrete dust everywhere, but more importantly, it solved the problem. Once again, the basement was dry and usable. Difficult though it had been, we had survived the pestilence and plagues and life carried on.

PAUL BUNYON I AM NOT...

E ven though I had passed the half century mark, I was still active and seldom hesitated to tackle a project. One fall afternoon, my husband decided he needed to cut a tree down in our back yard. It was a large tree and he asked if I would help. Sure, no problem...

He climbed the 20-foot ladder propped against the side of the tree and tied a long rope at the top of the tree. He assured me it would be a very simple task. He got down off the ladder and picked up his chain saw. My role was simply to pull the rope which was attached to the top of the tree and keep it taut and away from him so he could notch the tree and it would not fall on him. He also cautioned me not to let the tree fall on my head. Simple enough – I thought.

As he fired up the chain saw and began to carve the notch in the tree, I pulled on the rope as hard as I could. I was very careful not to let the tree move in the direction of my head. The tree began to lean away from him and from my head so all was good. However, I had paid very little attention to the location of my feet! With a loud crack, the tree came crashing down – RIGHT ON TOP OF MY LEFT FOOT! Ouch, that really hurt! I immediately fell to the ground, clutching my broken foot.

The next morning as I sat in my doctor's office looking at my swollen, purple foot, the doctor inquired, "…and just how did this happen?" After explaining the fiasco, he calmly asked how old I was. He already knew how old I was because it was on my chart, but he just HAD to ask. He then casually suggested that it might be time to retire from my tree-cutting career and let someone a little younger take over. (Never did like that doctor.)

CARPENTRY SKILLS

I've always been a "Project Person". If I wanted to create something or build something, I could usually figure out how to do it. Such was the case with my venture into carpentry.

I needed a few boards cut to a certain size to complete a craft project. I had solicited help in cutting the boards but all to no avail. Not being overly patient and really wanting to finish my project, I decided I would just do it myself.

Now I knew I needed a Circular Saw (or Skil Saw as we called them) to cut the boards and I knew what a Skil Saw was, but had I ever used one? NO, never. However, I had SEEN a Skil Saw being used and figured it couldn't be too difficult.

My craft table in the basement was the perfect worktable (I thought). I laid the 6' 2x4 boards across the table, picked up the Skil Saw, plugged it in and took a deep breath. I knew about the safety shield and figured out how to lower it over the blade, then I was ready to go. I turned the saw on and held on tight. It was a little harder to control than I thought it would be. Although I wanted to cut the boards straight, they ended up being cut on a slight angle. Oh well, that would just add character. And the slice on the table was hardly noticeable. Mission accomplished! Now I was an expert carpenter and I had mastered the infamous Skil Saw!

Having mastered the Skil Saw, I was ready for a bigger project – remodeling my kitchen cabinets! I always enjoyed watching Do It Yourself programs on TV and learned a lot (I thought). Anyway, on one of the programs, they were installing wide decorative crown molding at the top of the kitchen cabinets. It looked really good. Why, of course, I could do that!

My kitchen cabinets were very simple. They only had dental molding at the top. So, all I had to do was remove the dental molding and install the extra wide crown molding. Very simple. So, after one afternoon repeatedly climbing up and down the ladder, with lots of ceiling plaster falling in my hair, coupled with a few cuts and scrapes, VOILA! The dental molding was finally removed and lay crumpled in the floor.
Step One Complete!

Step Two: Off to the home supply store to buy the crown molding. I had watched enough DIY programs to know that installing crown molding required a miter saw to cut the corners in various angles. Well, somewhere out in the tool box was an old miter saw. I was pretty sure I could figure out how to use it. On another DIY program, I learned that there was such a thing as Styrofoam crown molding. I liked that idea. It wouldn't be nearly as heavy as wood crown molding to carry up the ladder. The folks on the DIY program said the Styrofoam had to be glued together. No problem. I'd ask the guy at home supply store

My husband reluctantly went with me to the store. As we were wandering around in the building material section, a middle- aged employee sporting his bright orange apron approached my husband and asked if he could help us. I replied that I was looking for Styrofoam crown molding. He ignored me and directed his response to my husband telling us where to find it. I then asked where the adhesive was located. I must have been invisible because once again he ignored me and directed his reply to my husband. By that time, I was a little annoyed when I asked him had he had any experience with these products. He stepped closer to my husband and asked him if he was planning a project with them.

OK, that was the last straw! I stepped in front of him and said, "No, my husband is not planning a project, I am and I'd like for you to help ME!" "Oh," he sheepishly replied, "It's just that we don't have many women doing these type projects." So much for Equal Opportunity for All...

Finally, I arrived home and unloaded my supplies – Styrofoam crown molding, adhesive, and tiny nails. I carefully measured the first piece and cut it exactly as measured. After climbing up the ladder to the top of the cabinets, I attempted to attached the Styrofoam to the wood cabinet with the tiny nails. Oops, did you know that hitting Styrofoam with a hammer leaves a serious indentation? Oh well, it was on the back side. Nobody would see it. Climbed down the ladder and cut the second piece of molding. That one had to be glued to the first piece. I carefully spread the adhesive to each end and stuck them together. I held it for a minute, then turned loose. Oh no, both pieces fell to the floor. How long was I supposed to hold the pieces together? Plan B – Glue the pieces together and nail them with those tiny nails. Nope, the nails came right out. OK, when all else fails; try Duct Tape.

It was a very long day but by nightfall, there was beautiful white extra wide decorative crown molding topping every cabinet in my kitchen. Did the installation work like the orange- aproned gentleman said it would? NO, IT DID NOT. However, learning to improvise is key to getting jobs done. Since the adhesive didn't work and the tiny nails didn't work, the only thing that worked was DUCT TAPE – and it worked beautifully. Who says you can't install Styrofoam crown molding with duct tape? Just be sure it is on the back side and nobody will see it. Ready for my next project (maybe).

Actually, I had already planned the next project. I wanted glass inserts on a few of the upper kitchen cabinet doors. Technically, I knew what needed to be done. First, the middle of the cabinet doors needed to be cut out and I needed some kind of saw for that.

Then I needed a router to make a groove for the glass panel to be attached. To complete the task, I needed narrow molding to secure the glass. Sounded pretty simple.

However, I made an executive decision and rather than risk spending time once again with the orange-aproned middle-aged home supply store person, I took the easy way out. Several weeks later, when my son, Robert was home from Connecticut, I casually asked if he would like to tackle the project. I assured him I was capable of doing it but thought he might enjoy it. (Yeah, right!) Anyway, he jumped right on it and 48 hours later, I had beautiful glass front cabinets in my newly remodeled kitchen. Family projects are such fun...

LEARNING TO PLAY THE PIANO

It had always been my dream to be able to play the piano but that dream was a long time in coming. My mother was an accomplished pianist. When I was a little girl, I used to sit on the floor of our living room behind her while she played. I loved hearing the piano and I desperately wanted to learn to play. I asked Mamma and Daddy if I could take piano lessons but they said we didn't have enough money.

No problem, I figured out a solution. There was a piano teacher at our local elementary school and students were allowed to leave their classroom and go to her music room for their lessons. The lessons cost $1.25 per week which was exactly what our school lunches cost per week. Since I was given lunch money each week, in my nine-year-old wisdom, I decided I would sign up for music lessons, pay for it with my lunch money and bring a sandwich to school for lunch.

After signing my name on the dotted line, I was ready to start lessons the following week. I had no idea the music teacher would contact my parents!!! Well, long story short, Mamma and Daddy were not happy with me. They did not like my plan and they quickly squelched the idea. I was terribly disappointed and didn't understand why Mamma and Daddy hadn't realized I had worked out everything and there would have been no extra cost to them. But they didn't and they made it clear that there was no room for discussion. Subject closed – or so they thought.

My love for the piano never dimmed but rather than being a young child, I was 61 years old when opportunity knocked again. As a Christmas gift that year, my youngest daughter, Allison gave me ten complimentary piano lessons. She was my teacher. I was thrilled! Why, I hadn't even applied for Medicare yet.

On the day of the first lesson, I didn't even know where Middle C was on the keyboard. I figured it had to be somewhere near the center since it was called Middle C. Allison was very patient as she explained the basic fundamentals. I was starting at Ground Zero and had SO MUCH to learn.

I practiced for an hour or more every day, anxious to show Allison how much I had learned. I had gone beyond our first lesson skills and was able to teach myself a few more skills. Allison was complimentary and laughingly called me an, "over-achiever."

Then came more new skills: reading the notes and fingering positions. Still practicing a couple of hours a day, I struggled to learn and recognize all of the notes. The treble notes weren't too difficult but the base notes just seemed to elude me. I had to figure a way to help me learn them. I was determined!

About that time, my husband and I took a road trip to Connecticut for my son, Robert's graduation from University of CT. Knowing I would not be able to practice the piano for a week, I devised my own system of "mental practicing" for much of the time we were on the road. The trip by car to and from CT took about four days so I had plenty of sitting time.

I mentally pictured each note on the staff, repeated its name and visualized its position on the keyboard. Then I mentally placed my hands on the keyboard and played the note. Strange as it sounds, the mental practicing actually helped me learn the notes. As the weeks and months passed, I continued practicing and managed to learn a few pieces of music.

By request from various family members, I performed my first (and only) piano recital at our Thanksgiving family gathering the following year. That was our annual Thanksgiving celebration at my Aunt Reba and Uncle Tommy Crawford's large log house in Carrollton, GA. Every year for forty years, our extended family had gathered together and enjoyed lots of delicious food and wonderful socializing. We usually had around fifty to sixty relatives and friends there.

In preparation for the infamous recital, a couple of my cousins had decorated the living room. A large chandelier adorned the top of the piano and a fluffy fur rug laid atop the piano bench. Certainly, fit for Liberace! For such an event, it seemed only fitting to pen a few verses.

FIRST PIANO RECITAL
By Ann Lovvorn Douglass

There was a young woman sixty-one years of age
Decided to perform on a living room stage
To tickle the ivories, a dream for years past
Giving it a try – sure hope my memory lasts

My hands a bit stiff – arthritis, you know
But, I'll keep on playing just a little bit slow
Surrounded by family, friends, and the like
Why playing the piano is like riding a bike

Once you learn, they say you'll never forget
But I'm not even sure where middle C is yet
So, my first recital, I'll play for you
In hopes you'll overlook mistakes I might do

RENOVATING THE LAKE CABIN

Sometimes life presents golden opportunities hidden in great disguises. Such was the case when daughter, Allison began sharing her vision of renovating her grandparents' lake cabin. The cabin, was located on the shores of Lake Allatoona.

The cabin was approaching its 50th year and was certainly past its prime. Several years of deferred maintenance had taken its toll. Much of the furniture was in sad condition. The property was leased from the Corp of Engineers and federal litigation prevented owners from tearing down the old cabin and rebuilding. Until the litigation was resolved, no structure could be added or removed, so the only alternative was to spruce up what they had.

Allison had grandiose plans for a top to bottom refurbishing and redecorating. She shared her plans with me and asked if I'd like to help. That, of course, was right up my alley. I jumped at the chance. I could hardly wait to get started! And so, the work commenced!

Our first task was to empty the cabin of all the old, dilapidated furnishings. My husband, Buddy supplied the pick-up truck and trailer but since he couldn't lift anything because of his heart condition, it was up to Allison and me to drag everything out of the cabin. It was truly a sight to see as we struggled with old mattresses and box springs that were damp, dirty, and moldy. Frequently, roach bugs and other vermin would scamper from under the mattresses we were carrying. Often, we laughed so hard, we almost dropped the vintage pieces.

After the cabin was empty, we began cleaning, repairing, painting and, beautifying. Allison's creative spirit was evident in her plans for every room. She chose a different theme for each room. She told me what her vision was for each room and I shopped for her. I took her digital camera to the stores with me and took pictures of things I thought she might want. Then, she would look at the pictures and make her purchasing decisions. When she told me what she wanted, I went back to the stores and made the purchases. She found pictures of the window treatments she wanted and I bought the fabric and did the sewing.

On the day she planned to purchase the new furniture, Allison asked us to meet her at the local discount store. Buddy and I arrived with truck with trailer in tow. She had not been able to get a baby sitter that day, so we had four-year-old Harrison and eight-month-old Lexi with us.

With Harrison's help, Allison made her selections. She bought a crimson red sofa and loveseat, a folding dining table with folding chairs, five box springs and four mattresses. The folks at the discount store insisted everything would fit in the truck and the trailer.

Buddy had multiple bungee cords stretched precariously over, under and around the mountain of furniture. The truck was filled, the trailer was filled and Allison's van was filled to the brim. I rode with Allison to help with the children. We told Buddy to drive slowly and we would follow him to the lake, which was only about fifteen minutes away.

We had driven little more than a couple of miles when we noticed the towering load of box springs shifting on the back of his truck. We held our breath. Then, suddenly as he rounded a curve in the road, the largest box spring fell off the trailer! Buddy, unaware he had lost part of his cargo, continued down the road. I told Allison to put on her emergency lights and stop the car in the road. I jumped out and dragged the box spring off to the side of the road. Then Allison pulled over to the side of the road. She called Buddy on her cell phone and told him the box spring had fallen off. He found a place to turn around and returned to the roadside where we were waiting. We managed to put the slightly damaged box spring back on the trailer.

We secured it the best we could and continued our journey.

Just a mile or two later, the load was once again shifting. We were quite fearful of a repeat performance. We called Buddy's cell phone and told him to stop as soon as he could. We needed more rope to secure the load. He made it to the nearest hardware store where he purchased more rope. With our two toddlers getting tired and hungry, we finally were able to secure the load fairly well. Once again, we continued our journey. It was an agonizingly slow trip, but we managed to arrive at our destination with everything reasonably intact. What should have been about a fifteen-minute drive to the lake cabin turned out to be an hour and a half. What a memorable trip!!!!

Our work continued for nine months. We worked a couple of days each week at the cabin from early morning to late evenings. When we weren't at the cabin working, we were working on the home projects: sewing, shopping, painting, refinishing hardware, etc.

The front room of the lake cabin was decorated in a Nantucket theme with bright red, white and blue. An old piece of driftwood found at the lake was hung above the bed. I found some large decorative fish lures which Allison attached to the driftwood.

The small living room was very rustic with a lot of her granddad's fishing memorabilia. We found his old metal tackle box in the bottom of one of the closets.

Allison emptied the box and meticulously cleaned all the old fishing lures. The window treatments in the living room were hung from tree branches with the fishing lures adding a very special touch. Allison filled the empty tackle box with dried flowers and set it on a table next to the window.

A punch of color was added to the kitchen. We painted the old brown cabinets a bold barn red. We removed all the old hardware and Allison refurbished every piece to its original copper color. A new cream-colored gas stove was purchased to replace the rusted avocado green relic from the past. New vinyl stick-and-peel floor tiles were added throughout the cabin.

The tiny front bedroom with bunk beds was designed with a tropical theme, complete with grass skirt window curtains. The bedspreads were brightly colored surf board motifs. I scanned the surf boards of the bedspread on my computer and printed replicas on computer fabric paper. Using the replicas, I made coordinating throw pillows for the beds.

The exterior was the last area to be updated. The screens on the porch were either badly ripped or missing altogether. We replaced the screens, repaired the damage above the screens and repainted.
One day when Allison was on a ladder at the top of the roof, she reached in to retrieve a rotted piece of wood and was greeted by a snarling raccoon! Her blood-curdling scream preceded her rapid descent from the ladder! I was on the other side of the cabin and thought she had fallen off the ladder. I raced around

the cabin to find her on the ground. Fortunately, she was not hurt, just a bit unnerved by the unexpected creature from above. Once all the repair work was completed, we painted the exterior white with sea-blue shutters and trim. It looked very nautical and so much better.

After the months of hard work, good times, creative fun and lots of laughter, the lake cabin was finally finished. The transformation was complete and was enjoyed for almost ten years. However, many structural and aesthetic issues remained due to the age of the building. So, Allison and her hubby, Lee continued petitioning the Corps of Engineers to allow them to tear down the old structure and rebuild a new cabin. At long last, permission was granted. The old structure was demolished and the new one built in its place. So, even though all the renovation work we did was ultimately demolished, the terrific memories will remain. What a great time we had!

GRANDMA IN A PICK-UP

It's amazing how some boys (and girls too) just have a knack for building cars and trucks. Such was the case with my oldest grandson, Seth. When Seth was just a toddler, he was at his dad's elbow whenever he was working on cars or trucks. I think he was genetically predisposed to automotive ingenuity. And it didn't hurt that Seth lived out in the country, surrounded by four-wheelers, tractors, and a variety of vehicles so he learned to drive at a very early age. Seth was probably dreaming of the day he would have his own vehicle even before he started first grade. By the time he was around 13 or 14, he and his dad were getting serious about Seth's future transportation.

Well, lo and behold, they stumbled upon a deal too good to pass up. They knew someone who had the remains of a pick-up truck they wanted to get rid of. Now, keep in mind, I said, "remains" of a pick-up truck. The truck was definitely not drivable. In fact, it was delivered in a mass of unidentifiable parts via front end loader to Seth's front yard. And then the fun began!

For the next couple of years, Seth and his dad worked diligently rebuilding that old truck. Part by part, as money allowed, it slowly began looking like a truck – a very big truck with very big tires. It must have been at least six feet off the ground. But, I guess that was fashionable as far as pick-ups went.

Finally, the big day arrived – Seth's 16th birthday. We went to his house to celebrate his birthday and specially to see the (almost) completed truck. "Hey, Grandma, wanna go for a ride in my truck?" Well, sure I wanted to go for a ride. There was no way I was going to miss that opportunity! Just one small problem – how to get in the truck. As I said, it was at least six feet off the ground and I couldn't jump that high. Seth didn't have any trouble getting in the truck but at sixteen, he was a bit more agile than a 64-year-old grandma. Never fear, Seth being the gentleman that he was, rushed over to the garage and brought out a plastic step ladder. Up I went. I managed to climb up and fall into the seat.

Looking around for the seat belt, I quickly realized there was none. Refurbishing had not progressed that far. Neither was there a windshield nor any other recognizable parts upon which to secure my body. Seth cranked the truck and I regretted that I had not brought my ear plugs. "Now, hold on, Grandma," said Seth. Hold on to what I almost said, but figured it best to be silent. There was some sort of metal something where the dashboard was supposed to be so I grabbed hold and prayed that it would stay connected.

Off we went down the bumpy dirt driveway. Seth was so proud and I was just praying I wouldn't fall out of the truck. We took a short ride and when we returned, Seth asked me how I liked it. I told him it was great. And indeed, it was great. Getting to share such a monumental moment with my terrific grandson was just the best thing ever – and I didn't even fall out of the truck.

GIFT BASKET EXCURSION

For many years, I enjoyed shopping and creating unique gift baskets. I donated hundreds of baskets to various charities and organizations. One particular charity started using one of my gift baskets as a door prize each week when their residents came for training. They said prior to giving the gift baskets as a door prize, the attendance had been poor. But once the residents learned about the gift baskets, attendance improved drastically! The participants were excited and eager to see who would win the basket each week.

One year as the Christmas season was approaching, I decided I wanted to do something I'd never done before. I wanted to host a Holiday Luncheon and Gift Basket Excursion for friends and family at my house.
I shopped for months (which I loved) and made about a hundred creative gift baskets. They were filled with household décor items, holiday treats, linens, etc.

As the plans began to gel in my mind, I was filled with excitement. I wanted to give everyone special gift baskets of their choice, but more importantly, I wanted to create an event that would be both fun and memorable. Thus, the seed was planted. I knew what I would do.

I made a special flyer with all the information and mailed it to friends and family. Everyone was invited to come for lunch and "shopping." When they arrived, they were given one hundred dollars in HOLIDAY BUCKS (fake money). What an incredible sight – the house filled with women shoppers and hundreds of HOLIDAY BUCKS! Each gift basket had a price tag attached to it and could be purchased with the HOLIDAY BUCKS the guests received. It was a shopping extravaganza but no real money was required. Everything was a gift.

As I was finishing the lunch preparations, all the guests were scurrying around checking out all the merchandise. "I want this one." "Don't take that one, it's mine." "Should I carry this out to my car now?" I decided it might be a good idea to provide some post-it notes for the ladies to lay claim to their chosen gifts.

Finally, after the guests had labeled their favorites, they sat down to lunch. I had home-made vegetable soup and chicken salad sandwiches served on my best Christmas china. For dessert, I had made a brown sugar pound cake and some German Chocolate brownies. We all enjoyed visiting and chatting during lunch, but shortly thereafter, the shopping frenzy had reignited.

It was interesting to note that of all the guests who were there, everyone knew someone, but no one (except me) knew everyone. Some were family members, some were friends from years past and some were fairly new acquaintances. Yet, everyone was very warm, personable and friendly. By the time they left, everyone knew everyone. It was such fun! I loved every minute and I think everyone had a wonderful time. It was a great holiday gathering!

MY FIRST PEDICURE

So, who says that pedicures are just for teenagers? At the age of sixty-three, my husband and I were getting ready to celebrate our twenty fifth wedding anniversary. Daughters, Angela and Allison had planned a wonderful luncheon with many friends and family joining us. I had shopped for a new outfit to wear – preferably one that would hide at least ten extra pounds. I "touched up" my golden locks with a little brownish tint and while hubby and I were doing some last-minute shopping, I suggested that I get a manicure and pedicure.

He looked puzzled and asked if I was sure I wanted to do that. I assured him I did and that I was ready to, **"*live on the edge*."** I might mention that manicures and pedicures were not part of my normal lifestyle. I had had one manicure in my life and that was before my junior-senior prom. I had **never** bared my feet for a pedicure.

We arrived at the manicure place and I told them what I wanted. The sweet little lady who spoke very little English motioned me to the chair with the foot washing station. I hesitantly sat on the edge of the chair. She motioned for me to take off my shoes and put my feet in the water. I dutifully complied. That wasn't so bad. The warm, soapy water bubbling around my feet felt pretty good.

Then, she asked if I wanted the regular or deluxe pedicure. Having no idea what the difference was, I tried to act suave and simply said, "Oh, I'll have the deluxe like always." I figured if I was going to do it, I'd do it right!

She began massaging my feet and ankles. Then, she looked as if she had seen something VERY strange. Through her broken English, she asked, "You have tanning lotion on feet?" Oh no, I had forgotten that to cover the purple varicose veins, I had sprayed the sunless tanning stuff on my feet and legs. The more she massaged, the whiter my feet and ankles became. Couldn't she just hurry up and finish?

But no, when the massage was finished, she lifted my feet onto the drain board and proceeded to dry them with a white towel. Why couldn't that towel have been beige or brown? It would have blended much better with the tanning lotion that was slowly dripping down my legs.

In the salon, there was a row of seven chairs and I was sitting slap dab in the middle. Needless to say, entertainment was provided for the other six ladies who were getting their pedicures. It's hard to believe but none of the other six ladies had availed themselves of the bronze sunless tanning lotion. Surely, I'm not the only female in the world who has been blessed with a few varicose veins! Well, when all was said and done, I did have beautiful toenails, but the purple roadmaps glimmered brightly against my white feet and ankles. I think I'll forget wearing sandals from now on. I hear brogans are becoming fashionable again.

100 YEAR FLOOD

September 20-21, 2009   Georgia's Record Flood

About mid-morning on that fateful Monday in September, I had gone downstairs to chat with my sister, Louise. She lived in our basement apartment. We were sitting in the sunroom watching the torrential downpour outside.   Looking out the window, what was normally the patio had morphed into a small lake.   As we chatted idly about how fortunate we were that the basement apartment was nice and dry, I noticed a small amount of water seeping under the doorway. Not too concerned, I suggested that Louise might want to put an old towel on the floor beside the seeping water.

As quickly as she put the towel on the floor, more water began coming in around the perimeter of the

90

room. Obviously, more than a towel was needed! I got the wet-dry vacuum from the far side of the basement and we began suctioning out the water. The water was coming in so rapidly, we couldn't keep up. The tank filled within a couple of minutes.

Emptying the tank was very difficult. It was much too heavy for either Louise or I to lift so we rolled it into the bathroom, got a pan and dipped the water out, pouring it into the bathtub. Needless to say, that was not very efficient but it was the best we could do.

With the water pouring into the apartment, I decided another approach might work better. Looking outside at the incredible amount of water raging down the back yard, I concluded it would be more advantageous if I could somehow re-route the water to flow away from the house. Obviously, I was a bit naïve in my flood control solutions but it seemed like a good idea at the time.

I grabbed a jacket, put on an old pair of tennis shoes and rushed outside. The rain was blinding as I grabbed a pick, shovel and rake! The water was knee deep and the wind was so strong, I had to hold on to trees to keep from being swept away! Making my way to the lower end of the yard, I quickly began trying to dig a trench to redirect the raging water. The rain was so fierce; I could barely see what I was digging!

I worked as long as I could, but finally conceded the force of the water was stronger than I was! Looking like a drowned rat, I reluctantly gave up and returned inside. Meanwhile, Louise had continued to use the wet-dry vacuum to try to hold back the tide of water coming inside. Water was now flowing inside all around the perimeter of the basement. It was a losing battle. The water couldn't be contained!

Our Aunt Carolyn owned an empty condo in Marietta. She graciously offered Louise a temporary home while hers was under water so Louise packed what she needed and moved to the condo. That became her beautiful home away from home for the immediate future.

After two stormy days and dumping up to twenty inches of rain on many parts of Cobb County, the heavy storms catapulted Georgia into a record breaking flood. Ten people lost their lives and countless more had to be rescued. More than twenty thousand homes sustained major flood damage. All told, the storm did an estimated five hundred million dollars in damages to the state.

When the rains finally subsided, the work began to try to dry out the basement so that it was livable again. With the help of Grandson, Seth we worked diligently suctioning out the water with the wet-dry vacuum. We were able to remove most of the water. The following day, I finished extracting the water and steam cleaned all the carpet. The flooding we experienced in our home was challenging and somewhat frightening, but considering the devastation statewide, I felt extremely fortunate. Although our basement apartment was out of commission for a while and our beautifully landscaped yard looked like a back hoe had gone berserk in it, there was no loss of life nor any injuries (except for my sore back). We were fortunate and had much to be thankful for.

FLASHING BLUE LIGHTS

Grandchildren are by far one of life's most precious gifts and I've always felt it was very important to set a good example in all that we do. Getting to spend time with my grandchildren has always been a joy.

My four-year-old granddaughter, Lexi had spent the day with me and we had enjoyed many fun projects during the day. Her mom had asked me to pick up the two older siblings, Ashley and Harrison at their bus stop that afternoon.

Well, as sometimes happens when having fun with little ones, time gets away from us. Such was the case that afternoon. While driving across town to pick up the other grandchildren at their bus stop, I was running a little late and my foot was a bit heavy on the accelerator. Suddenly, young Lexi said, "Grandma, what are those flashing blue lights on the car behind us?"

Oh dear, I was in trouble but I did not want Lexi to be frightened. I slowly pulled over to the side of the road and stopped the car In her four-year-old inquisitiveness, Lexi asked why I was stopping. Taking a deep breath as I rolled the car window down, I calmly told Lexi that the nice policeman wanted to see my driver's license and to talk to me. "Well, what does he want to talk about? Will he talk to me too?" (Oh, the innocence of children.)

Drawing on my years of experience teaching young children, I explained that he wanted to talk about driving a car and how we should drive safely and not drive too fast... "Well, how do you know how fast you are supposed to drive," asked Lexi. I explained that there were signs beside the road that told how fast to drive. Then the policeman inquired, "Mam, do you know how fast you were driving?" As I'm attempting to explain to the policeman that I was running late to pick up my two other grandchildren from their bus stop, Lexi pops up asking if I had seen the signs on the road. Now I was dealing with double interrogation! I guess the policeman took pity on me since I was going to have to explain to a four-year-old why I had not obeyed the signs on the road. Fortunately, I only received a warning and did not have to forfeit my license so I continued my way.

That evening, when I took the grandchildren home, their dad was waiting for them. No sooner had we gotten inside the house than Lexi said, "Dad, guess what? A nice policeman with a flashing blue light on his car stopped behind us. He and Grandma talked about driving a car. There were signs on the road telling Grandma how fast to drive but I guess she didn't see them. The policeman was very nice. I liked him."

Would I ever be entrusted with the care of my grandchildren again???

50th HS REUNION

I was busy with plans for our 50th high school reunion. It was a good opportunity for me to stay active since the loss of my husband the previous year. I had been unexpectedly thrust into widow-hood and life was filled with many challenges and adjustments. How I ended up on the Reunion Planning Committee was another story indeed. It all began months after the death of my husband...

Autumn had transitioned into chilling winter then spring slowly emerged. On a beautiful sunny day, my sister, Louise invited me to go to the Sprayberry High School alumni luncheon with her. She insisted I needed to, "get out more and be around people." Going to an alumni luncheon was the last place I wanted to go. I thanked her kindly and declined. It was difficult enough to engage in social niceties with the clerk at the local grocery store. I couldn't imagine having to chat with dozens of alumni that I hadn't seen in years. However, she wouldn't take no for an answer. To appease her, I decided I'd meet her there, eat a quick bite of lunch then make a speedy exit. Little did I know that she was God's messenger and that day would be the beginning of a beautiful journey.

Trying hard to swallow a few bites of lunch, I continued to glance at my watch, waiting for the socially acceptable minutes to pass so that I could gracefully exit. Finally, there was a slight lull in conversation and I stood up, preparing to leave. Simultaneously, one of the alumni also stood up. He wanted to make an announcement. Why had I not left a few minutes earlier so I wouldn't have to sit through whatever he was going to say? Politely, I returned to my seat and watched the second-hand circle the face of my watch. Whatever he had to say, I wasn't interested.

Plans were being formulated for our 50th class reunion. A group of alumni had formed a small committee but they needed more help. His words fell on deaf ears as I stared out the large window of the restaurant, idly watching cars traveling on the busy highway. However, between God's tugging at my heart and Louise's encouragement, I agreed to volunteer. The committee was scheduled to meet the following week.

I had a terrible knot in my stomach as I arrived for the committee meeting. Several cars were parked on the street and I could see people inside the living room. I really didn't want to be there but I forced one foot in front of the other and soon I felt the coolness of the doorbell beneath my finger. By evening's end, all the tasks had been assigned with one exception. No one wanted to create the Class Memory Book. Feeling that I should be willing to do SOMETHING, I volunteered.

In the weeks that followed, I sent each alumnus a questionnaire to gather current information to be shared in the book. When I began receiving the responses, something incredible happened! One of the responses almost jumped off the page. I know it must have been Divine Intervention. The response was from fellow-classmate, Duane Douglass. His words were very brief, offering little personal information. He said he was retired from the U.S. Army, lived near Columbus, GA and had written two books of poetry. I was also a writer and had written a couple of books of poetry so I sent him a brief email asking if he would bring a copy of his book to the reunion. He quickly responded that he would.

After months of work and planning, the evening of the reunion finally arrived. I was sitting at the registration table when I saw Duane walk in with a book in his hand. He came over, handed me his book of poetry and hugged me briefly. I had not seen him in fifty years. I remembered he had beautiful eyes when we were in high school and he still did. We talked for a few minutes. He told me his wife of thirty-six years had passed away the previous year. We talked briefly about the loss of our spouses. Our conversation lasted less than five minutes then he disappeared in the crowd.

It was late that night after the reunion was over before I returned to my room at the hotel. About 2:30 AM the following morning, I took out his book of poetry and began to read. When the book was finished, I smiled and thanked God for bringing a smile back to my life.

Arriving home, the day after the reunion, I once again read Duane's book. What was it about Duane Douglass that I couldn't get out of my mind??? I waited until the following day and sent an email thanking him for the book. Almost immediately, I received a reply. He said he was just sitting down to send me an email when he received mine. My heart skipped a beat!

Very quickly, the daily emails between Duane and I bridged the hundred-mile distance between us. The magnetism of our friendship inextricably connected us. Neither of us could explain the strong attraction, but we both felt it. I was convinced God had a special plan for us. The long emails soon morphed into on-line chats and phone calls. Duane asked if he could come to see me and take me out to dinner on my birthday. I felt like a nervous sixteen-year-old and told him I'd love to go out to dinner with him.

Duane arrived at 7AM on Thursday, August 25th for my birthday. I was pacing the floor in anticipation of his visit. I hadn't slept at all the night before. We had never even held hands and here he was at my house for my birthday. He brought me two dozen beautiful red roses. He stayed in town until Monday morning. A special friendship was becoming even more special. We could not explain it but we knew that it was real!

We had begun an unbelievable journey; the destination yet to be determined.

After Duane returned to his home, a hundred miles away, we traversed the distance through emails, telephone, on-line chats and notes. The incredible feeling that had grown into love had skyrocketed at lightning speed. What was the protocol? We weren't teenagers although we both felt like it. What we wanted was to be together, to share our lives. We had both experienced sadness and grief, losing our mates but God had given us a special love to be shared.

A cozy log cabin nestled in the North Georgia Mountains – what could be a more perfect setting for our honeymoon!!! Surrounded by our families and friends, Duane and I were married just three and a half months after our High School Reunion. As we drove north to the cabin on Interstate 575, many cars blew their horns and waved at our creatively decorated "Just Married" car. Some drivers did a double-take when they saw the newly-weds were a bit older than the average couple. The beginning of our new life together was God's gift awaiting us, "...just around the corner."

VALENTINE'S DAY SNOWFALL

My husband, Duane and I were living in our North Georgia cabin for six months while our new home was being built in Kennesaw, GA. We loved the mountains and the beauty of the changing seasons. That winter, we were blessed with an abundance of snow – beautiful, white, fluffy snow!

The date was February 14th, Valentine's Day and we were completely snowed in. Getting out of our long, winding driveway was impossible. We didn't mind being snowed in. We had a nice warm fire in the fireplace, plenty of food and a generator in case we lost power.

However, Duane, being the romantic that he was, had not been able to purchase flowers or a Valentine card for me. But never fear, his creative mind was working overtime. He bundled up in his warmest coat and hat and ventured out in the snow. He spent almost an hour stomping out a beautiful Valentine's message in the snow. Footprint by footprint, he meticulously wrote, I LOVE YOU! in the snow. Then, he drew a picture for me of a crimson red rose. So, I did indeed receive the most special Valentine card and flowers that I had ever gotten! Best Valentine's Day ever!

11 TOILETS IN ONE DAY

Fortunately, our beloved cabin in the North Georgia mountains, DID have indoor plumbing. The little guest cottage on site also had indoor facilities. However, they were all a bit outdated – the two toilets in the cabin and one toilet in the guest cottage. In an effort to update the facilities, we decided to replace all the toilets.

Off we went to the local home store. We were in luck. Toilets were on sale that day so we bought three shiny new white toilets. The salesman loaded the three toilets in the back of our blue pick-up truck and we headed up the mountain to our cabin. We arrived safely and Duane unloaded all three heavy toilets, putting them in their respective locations.

The plumber was on site and all was going well until I realized – the sinks and bathtubs in the bathrooms were not WHITE, they were IVORY! Neither the Appalachian plumber nor my sweet husband realized that we simply **could not** have mis-matched pieces in the bathrooms. No, I was not hysterical, I was simply attempting to explain how important color and design were in every home. I don't think they got it at all but it was easier for them to simply agree than to attempt World War III.

Fortunately, Duane was strong and in good health and he was able to load the three very heavy white toilets into the back of his truck for the return trip to the home store. With sales receipt in hand, Duane explained to the Customer Service Representative that he needed to exchange the three white toilets for three ivory toilets. No problem. The kind salesman exchanged the three toilets and loaded ivory toilets in the back of his truck.

Back up the mountain to our cabin and Duane unloaded the three **very heavy ivory toilets** and put them in their respective locations. The Appalachian plumber still waiting patiently... Oh no, what was that??? One of the toilets was damaged. By this time, Duane was not smiling but he struggled to get the damaged very heavy ivory toilet back down the stairs and into the back of his truck.

Off to the home store AGAIN. Reporting to the Customer Service Desk with sales receipt in hand, he explained that one of the toilets was damaged and he needed to return it and get another one. The salesman, who Duane knew on a first name basis by then, said he was so sorry but that store did not have any more ivory toilets but he would be glad to check with some other stores locations. Finally, he located one in a nearby town about 20 miles south.

Knowing it would be dangerous to his health if he returned to the cabin without the ivory toilet, Duane headed south to the other home store. Fortunately, they had the ivory toilet waiting for him. The salesman loaded it into his truck and once again he headed back up the mountain to the cabin. I smiled when he arrived with the toilet in the back of the truck. He didn't smile. Huffing and puffing, for the eleventh time that day, he lifted the very heavy ivory toilet out of the truck and lugged it back up the stairs. The Appalachian plumber was still waiting patiently... Oh, thank you so much. I really loved the new toilets! I tried to show my appreciation but somehow, I think it fell on deaf ears.

LET'S GO TO THE BEACH

Duane and I were sitting on the loveseat having our morning coffee as we always did. I had been feeling a little stressed lately after almost four months in our North Georgia cabin. We were living in our cabin while our new home in Kennesaw was under construction. Looked like it would be another two to three months before our new home was finished.

For some strange reason, I felt an intense urge to go to the beach, to walk along the sandy shore watching the ocean waves rolling in. I turned to Duane and said, "Let's go to the beach." He looked a little puzzled, probably because it was the middle of winter but then smiled and said okay. We quickly packed a few clothes and off we went.

We decided to go to Pawley's Island, SC. I had been to Pawley's a couple of times but Duane had never been there. We drove most of the day and arrived at our hotel about 7:30 pm. It was dark and raining so we didn't go to the beach that night.

The next morning, we awoke to a beautiful day filled with sunshine. After breakfast at the hotel, we headed down Hwy. 17 to the Pawley's Island Causeway.   As we drove all around the island, Duane was impressed with the many beautiful birds. We parked near the beach and walked down to the ocean. We had planned to walk barefoot on the sand but it was about 45 degrees and very windy so we opted to keep our shoes on.

There were only a few other people on the beach. It was very beautiful, serene and peaceful as we walked hand in hand. We picked up a few seashells and looked for pieces of driftwood. Walking along the beach was a wonderful stress reliever.

After we left the beach, we drove to Georgetown. We discovered a beautiful fishing and observation pier jutting out over the costal waterway. We walked out on the pier nodding and saying hello to the few fishermen beside the rails.

About mid-way, Duane stopped and said, "There must be an angel here." There was a small white feather lying beside us. I picked up the feather, experiencing a very warm feeling as I did. I put the feather in my pocket.   Then Duane said, "Look at the clouds. Do you see that?" The clouds looked just like an angel.   He took a picture of the clouds. I do believe there are angels among us here on earth. Perhaps, that was our angel!

 Just as we were getting ready to leave, I saw three sea gulls near the water. I snapped a couple of pictures but wanted to get closer. Very slowly, I walked toward them. As I neared them, two of the gulls moved away from the third. The lone bird was content for me to get closer and closer. As the lens of the camera captured his image, his wings expanded as he flew toward the ocean. The photograph was beautiful – sea gull in flight, reflection on the water while the other two birds had journeyed off together. Sometimes, I read a great deal into everyday happenings but perhaps this was more than just sea gulls on the beach. I think it may have been...

After a nice lunch in Georgetown, we enjoyed a scenic walk through town and along the waterfront. We returned to our hotel for a short rest then drove around enjoying the sights. We explored Merrill's Inlet and Myrtle Beach then had a great dinner at a local restaurant on Surf Side Beach.

Yep, sometimes you just need to go to the beach...

ANIMATED HALLOWEEN

Halloween was always such a festive time of year, welcoming in the autumn colors and chill in the air. Many small towns celebrate by having contests to see who can design and build the most creative vignettes featuring scarecrows or Halloween dummies. Such was the case in Blairsville, GA. The town square was filled with myriads of fun-filled, creative vignettes.

As Duane and I walked around the Square, we saw a vignette of a very "robust" lady dressed in a hot pink outfit reclining on a park bench. Around the corner, perched on bales of straw were a couple of large black birds with straw protruding out the edges of their shirt sleeves. Gigantic straw hats covered their heads. As we made our way through the throngs of mountain folks who were sharing laughs and smiles, I spotted an unusual vignette.

Across the street, beside a local cafe' were two middle-aged dummies dressed in ragged jeans and faded plaid shirts. As we walked closer, I was in awe. Someone had created a vignette with ANIMATED characters. The two men were smoking cigarettes. Their mouths moved as though they were talking to each other. Then, they looked away toward the crowds. One of them smiled and propped his foot on a nearby chair. It looked so real. I could almost smell the smoke. In my excitement, I exclaimed loudly to Duane that he needed to get closer so he could see the animated characters.

Now, in my own defense, it might be helpful to mention that that incident occurred prior to my having cataract surgery. My vision was not very good and my night vision was even worse.

Anyway, as I was coaxing Duane over to see that unbelievable feat of animation, you'll never guess what happened. One of the "dummies" turns to his friend, shakes his hand and walks down the street (still smoking his cigarette). Oh, my word! The people around us are not looking at the animated characters, they are looking at ME. I whispered to Duane that it might be time for us to go home. Oh dear, I hope nobody recognized me!

SNAKES!!!

Pretty shamrocks, cascading Creeping Jenny, pungent basil, oregano and evergreens – what a beautiful garden. Well, all of those are beautiful, but those pesky weeds that seem to thrive are not so beautiful.   So, as every good gardener knows, somebody has to remove the bad stuff so we can enjoy the good stuff. Such was our task one sunny afternoon as hubby, Duane and I donned garden gloves and set to work.

Now Duane's an avid gardener and outdoorsman. He's in his element when the earthy soil is coating his skin and sweat is dripping. Not only that, he's on a first name basis with all the bugs, snakes, worms and flying what-evers in the garden. Me, on the other hand – not so much. About the only living creatures that I love in a garden are butterflies. Bugs, snakes, worms or flying creatures do not bring me joy. Suffice it to say, I am *somewhat frightened* of snakes – makes no difference if they're a garden snake or a Black Mamba. I honestly don't know the difference.

While we were digging weeds in the garden, Duane cautioned me to be careful about snakes, telling me certain ones were poisonous. I told him there was no way I was going to get close enough to a snake to tell if it had a yellow diamond, purple spots, a pointed head or any other distinguishing characteristics.

The more he cautioned me, the more uneasy I became but I didn't want to act like a sissy and run away from the garden. So, I decided I would convince myself that there were no snakes out there, therefore I was safe! All I needed to do was redefine the word snake. Since worms are long and round just like snakes, in my head, I decided anything that was long and round would simply be a very large worm, not a snake. And you know what? It worked! When that long skinny thing came slithering on the ground, I simply told myself that it was a big, fat worm. Worms are much nicer than snakes. My first instinct was to decapitate the creepy-crawler, but I resisted the urge and moved away.

Although, my solution worked reasonably well for me, I wouldn't recommend it for others. You see, I have never been blessed with perfect vision and often I truly cannot identify what I am seeing. So, if indeed the creepy crawly that came slithering along was a Black Mamba, perhaps another plan of action might be preferable.

ALL CAME TUMBLING DOWN

Whenever we spent time at our beloved mountain cabin, we always seemed to be involved in projects. That particular weekend, the project of choice was building retainer walls around our gardens and walkways. Of course, that necessitated a trip to our local home store to purchase the needed lumber for the walls.

We selected lots and lots of eight feet long 2X4's. Actually, there were only forty-six. It just seemed like a lot more! Since we no longer had our pick-up truck to haul the lumber up the mountain to our cabin, we used our white SUV. When the back seats were folded down, there was a lot of room, so one by one all forty-six 2X4's were hoisted into the back of the SUV. There was just one small problem. They were eight feet long which was about two feet longer than the back of the SUV but Duane assured me everything would be fine. I suggested that we might want to secure them with some bungee cords to keep them from falling out but

Duane said that wasn't necessary since we only had about two miles to go.

So, off we go with the tail ends of forty-six 2X4's sticking out the back of our SUV. Oh, by the way, did I mention that our cabin was located at the top of a mountain? Driving very slowly, we turned into the steep road leading up to our driveway. Now, I was sitting in the passenger's seat twisted around attempting to hold on to forty-six 2X4's when I felt them begin to slide. I grasped them tighter, but all to no avail. Suddenly, they slipped and KERPLUNK – out they all went from the back of the SUV. Oh, my word! Duane stopped the SUV and we got out to assess the damages. 2 X4's were all over the road. Sure, hope the neighbors didn't see us.

We were less than a quarter of a mile from our driveway but it was all up hill. We knew we couldn't put all the 2X4's back in the SUV or they would just fall out again. So, we put a few in and I held them as tight as I could while we traversed the hill. We delivered those to the cabin and returned for another load. A couple more trips and we finally got all the lumber safely delivered to the cabin. Turned out to be quite an adventure and after we got over the initial shock of all the lumber falling out of the SUV, we laughed so hard, tears were falling. The moral of this story is never try to put forty-six 2X4's in the back of an SUV without the benefit of bungee cords!

FOOT SURGERY WAKE UP

Foot pain is not fun! In fact, it can be downright debilitating. Surely, the pain will just go away in time – or so I thought. But, unfortunately, it didn't so I finally made the appointment with the local podiatrist.

The good doctor spent a little while probing and examining my feet. Yes, I said, "feet" meaning not just one foot, but two feet, both of which were in serious pain. At the conclusion of the examination, the doctor determined that I needed surgery on both feet.

Since I was an educator by profession, my appointment calendar was always guided by the local school calendar. I was told both surgeries would require about six to eight weeks recovery time. Being the efficient person that I was, I concluded that having the surgery done on both feet at the same time and scheduling during the summer months when I was not working would be most expedient. (Knowing what I know now, I probably should have re-visited that decision.)

On the scheduled day in the sweltering summer heat, I appeared at the appointed time at the surgical center. After completing a mountain of paperwork and signing 500 different forms assuring them I would not file a lawsuit even if both of my feet fell off or worse, I was taken back to the operating room.

Amid the chill of the room, I was asked to change my sartorial splendor and put on the lovely hospital gown. "No undergarments and gown ties in the back." Why must they always sound so military-ish. A little kindness would have gone a long way. Oh well, to them it was just a job. Next came the anesthesiologist. He was much nicer as he assured me it was just going to be a little sting as he pushes the needle into my vein. Ouch – felt like a hornet's sting! Then the IV drip is started and he assured me I would feel very sleepy. He asked me to start counting backward from ten to zero. I never got to zero, four was the best I could do but by then I was snoozing in grand style.

Now before I went to sleep, I remembered that there were several people in the operating room with me: the doctor, anesthesiologist, and a couple of nurses. Once I went to sleep, I had no idea how many were there or even what they were all doing. I really didn't care either. However, all of a sudden, I was no longer asleep. I was wide awake!

Lying on the table, I remained very still. I moved my eyes in all directions trying to clear my head and discern exactly where I was. I heard voices and looked down toward my feet. The doctor and a couple of nurses were laughing chatting away. They were operating on my feet but I couldn't feel anything. Was I really awake or just dreaming? OK, I had to figure that out so I propped up on my elbows and said, "Hello". Oh, my word, you would have thought the Almighty Himself had spoken!

The doctor looked at me and yelled that I was awake. I assumed from his reaction that I was supposed to still be enjoying naptime. Suddenly, the nice anesthesiologist reappears and adjusts the IV drip. Perhaps he had just been out on a coffee break. Here we go again with that backward counting. 10, 9, 8 z-z-z-z-z-z-z I don't know how much time passed before the nurse was touching my shoulder, telling me it was time to wake up, that the surgery was finished. Still a little groggy, I mentioned to her that I had awakened during the surgery. Oh no, she assured me that that didn't happen but I knew better. They might want to schedule their coffee breaks after surgery next time rather than during surgery.

Well, as I mentioned earlier, I had surgery on both feet at the same time. When I left the surgical center in a wheelchair of course, I was wearing two gigantic "boots", each of which extended from my toes to my knees. The doctor said I should not attempt much walking for the first few weeks. That was all well and good, but we didn't discuss exactly how I was supposed to ambulate to answer nature's calls. To make a long story short, with the assistance of beloved family members, I was able to survive those weeks of convalescence but my advice to anyone contemplating surgeries on both feet simultaneously, I would strongly suggest you reconsider. Believe me, it's not much fun!

CAMDEN, ALABAMA

Have you ever planned a special birthday trip only to have it turn out VERY differently from your plans? Well, I have! Hubby, Duane and I are both avid quilt lovers and had recently fallen in love with the Quilts of Gee's Bend. We decided to celebrate our birthdays (mine August 25th and his August 28th) by a trip to Gee's Bend to see the quilters.

We had become enamored with the Quilts of Gee's Bend after seeing them in a local exhibit. Gee's Bend is located inside the curve of the Alabama River just south of Selma near a rural community called Camden, Alabama. Gee's Bend is one of America's most isolated communities, being linked to the outside world by a single road which remained unpaved until the 1960's. The original residents were slaves working on cotton plantations. Later generations were tenant farmers living in log cabins they built themselves.

The quilts of Gee's Bend were utilitarian quilts made to keep the families warm and protect against cold and drafty cabins. The scraps of fabric, mostly feed sacks, muslin or wool were a tapestry of colors. The women who created these treasures were the poorest of the poor – never imagining their quilts would be of value. But, their treasures were discovered and their value skyrocketed.

On route to Gee's Bend, Duane "surprised" me with a little side trip. Thinking we might be going to see some beautiful flower gardens or eat at a fancy restaurant, I was filled with exciting anticipation. We finally arrived at a heavily wooded location with a small building nestled among the bushes. Where was he taking me??? We got out of the car as I was inquiring what this surprise might be. With a big smile, he replied, "Just wait. You will love it!" Opening the door of the small white building, I was greeted by a ginormous alligator! Fortunately, it was no longer of this world. It was stuffed and displayed on a very large table. The sign below it identified it as the largest Stokes Alligator ever found in the Alabama River in Wilcox County. It was 15.9 feet long and 1,1011.5 pounds

 Words cannot express the joy I felt about my "surprise!" Love it? Not exactly, but I tried to appear interested...After all, how often does one get to see a stuffed 15.9-foot alligator on a birthday celebration venture???

Once the alligator excitement subsided, we continued our journey toward Camden. We drove for miles and miles on country roads. Absent were the familiar array of fast food eateries, strip malls and service stations. We had chosen to travel back roads rather than interstate highways. As mid-afternoon approached, we began searching for a nice place to have a picnic.

Amid lush green trees along the roadside, we spied an old boarded-up church nestled among the trees. We pulled off the road and parked in the grass. Nearby was an old, cracked concrete circular picnic table. How perfect! We leisurely spread our red checked plastic tablecloth over the rough concrete table top and opened the picnic basket. Delicious cheese, red cherries, grapes and crackers were the perfect lunch. Following lunch, we explored the vintage church, took a few pictures and continued our journey. Soon we arrived in Camden, Alabama.

The only access to Gee's Bend was by ferry and the next scheduled trip was not until the next morning so we decided we would find a nice hotel for the night, then go out to a nice restaurant to celebrate our birthdays. Now Camden, Alabama was about the size of a postage stamp. I think the roads were paved but the dust was so thick, I couldn't be positive. As we rode through the dusty maze, there were no hotels in sight so we stopped at a local service station and inquired. The young girl behind the counter assured us there were two nice establishments, directly across the road from each other. They were about three miles, "down yonder."

Back in the car heading down yonder, we finally spotted two hotel signs – one on each side of the road. They looked equally, "luxurious." Pulling into the dirt parking lot of the one on our side of the road, we looked around surveying the facility. There was one old rusty pick-up truck in the parking lot and a swimming pool filled with concrete. Well, not exactly what we were expecting or hoping for, but I was sure the rooms would be nice and cozy. WRONG!!!

As we were unloading our luggage from the car, a gentleman walked up to me. He had long, straggly hair, a beard that probably had never been trimmed and ragged jeans and shirt. I took a deep breath, wishing Duane would return to the car. The gentleman said, "Hey there mam. You ain't from here, is you?" Trying to be polite, I replied no, that I wasn't from there to which he inquired, "Where you lives?" I told him just north of Atlanta. Then he smiled and said he hoped I had a nice visit and that I had chosen a really nice hotel to stay in. (Well, I certainly learned a lesson. Never judge a book by its cover. The gentleman turned out to be a very nice "gentleman" after all.)

Once inside the room, Duane put our luggage on the bed and locked the outside door. Now, I suppose the maid had inadvertently missed our room when she had cleaned earlier that day. I'm trying to give her the benefit of the doubt. Oh well, a little dirt never killed anyone.

While surveying the room, we noticed there was about a 4" gap at the bottom of the door – certainly big enough for critters to come visiting. In my earlier years, I had some wilderness camping experiences out in the woods but wasn't interested in repeating it that night. Coming up with a brilliant solution, Duane went back to the car and got his long umbrella and his rain coat. Once back inside, he wrapped the coat around the umbrella and stuffed it into the gaping hole. OK, problem solved.

Then I decided to check out the bathroom. Oops, I sat down on the throne and the seat fell off! It was not attached – and I don't mean it was loose – it was NOT ATTACHED at all! It was just sitting on top of the toilet. Well, Duane always kept a tool box in the car so he removed the raincoat wrapped umbrella from the gaping door and retrieved his tools. He returned to our room, stuffed the raincoat covered umbrella back under the door and began working on the toilet seat. Shortly thereafter, the toilet seat was properly attached.

The hour was getting late and our stomachs were growling so off we went for a nice dinner. WRONG AGAIN! There were no restaurants in Camden and the next best thing was a small IGA grocery store. OK, we were sure to find something to eat. The folks in the IGA were all very nice and friendly. We managed to find a few snacks that would suffice. Returning to our room, we once again wrapped the long umbrella with

Duane's raincoat and stuffed it in the gaping crack under the door.

I tried to wash the top of the small table in our room to remove the sticky whatever. (I didn't really want to think about what that sticky stuff might have been.) Covering it with our red plastic tablecloth, we spread our snacks on the table and prepared for our gourmet birthday dinner. Not the birthday we'd planned, but one of our most memorable.

Early the next morning, we boarded the ferry to cross the Alabama River. We couldn't have asked for a more beautiful day and the ferry ride was wonderful – so peaceful and relaxing. Finally, we arrived at Gee's Bend. As we drove through the impoverished community, it was sad to see such poverty in our world today.

We were anxious to find the Community House and see the women of Gee's Bend quilting those wonderful quilts. At last we found the Community House amidst the tall, overgrown grass on the side of the road but it was empty. No sign of life anywhere. After making several phone calls, we discovered that the women only quilted at certain times and the time we were there was not one of those times. It was several months later before they were scheduled to quilt. That was very disappointing since that was the purpose of our trip. However, as we drove home later that day, we concluded that we had indeed taken one of the best birthday trips ever. It's often what we haven't planned that super-cedes what we did plan that makes for a wonderful celebration.

BUBBLE TEA

Not long ago, teenage granddaughter Ashley inquired if I had ever had "Bubble Tea". Thinking it must be some sort of fizzy, carbonated tea, I told her no, that I had not. Nothing would do but that I try it. So, the next time we were in Marietta, we went to the Bubble Tea place to sample the very popular beverage. Popular that is with all the chic, cute younger set. I didn't see a single other person in the establishment that looked even close to the, "grandma stage of life."

Ashley was kind enough to order for me and I was sure whatever she selected would be fine. When I was handed the cup, I didn't see a single bubble. However, there was a giant size straw stuck in the lid of the cup. A little awkward but it was okay. As I inhaled through the giant straw, suddenly something foreign swooped into my mouth. I didn't know whether to spit it out or try to chew it. It was round and tasted like a gummy bear candy. That, I was told was what the bubbles were. They were referred to as "pearls". In reality, they were round balls of tapioca. Now, I have always loved tapioca pudding but believe me, that was NOT pudding! Trying to be a good sport, I slowly sipped my bubble tea (avoiding as many, "pearls" as possible) as we continued our walk around the Marietta Square.

Several months later, another granddaughter, Ansley decided to look for a part-time job during her summer break from college. Guess where she was hired? Yep, she was offered a job at none other than Bubble Tea. After only a few days on the job, her boss was so impressed with her, she was promoted to cashier. That would be the person who takes the customers' orders and their money.

Well, as most grandparents do, we always like to support and encourage our grandchildren in all their endeavors. So, one sunny afternoon, Duane and I were walking around the Marietta Square and decided to stop at Bubble Tea and see Ansley at work. The place was swamped with all the younger set – some sitting at the tables engaged with their digital devices and others lounging on the sofas socializing with friends.

There was a long line of patrons waiting to place their orders so we took our place at the end of the line. During our wait time, I unobtrusively surveyed the crowd and saw no one appearing to be over 25 years old. Oh well, I was 25 once – long, long ago. Finally, it was our turn to place our order. Ansley was delightful as she smiled and asked what we would like. Duane chickened out and just asked for a plain ice tea. Trying to be as chic as a grandma can be, I told Ansley I'd like a bubble tea. "What kind?" she inquired. Good heavens, I had no idea there were dozens and dozens of different kinds so I suavely replied, "Well, which would you recommend?" After agreeing to her recommendation, we paid for our order and were told to wait in the next line, that they would call our name when our order was ready. So, we retreated to a group of 20-somethings and waited. Other names were called: Mike, Betty, Lisa, Mary...... Finally, over the loud speaker, we hear, "Grandma". Obviously, I was the only "Grandma" in the room so I walked over to the counter – my face matching the red cup in my hand.

All in all, as I pondered the situation later that day. I felt very proud of granddaughter, Ansley who had been brave enough to write Grandma on the ticket. Yes, she knew my name but to her I had always been and would always be, "Grandma". What could be better that that – not even bubble tea!!!

COME FLY WITH ME

My son, Robert earned his private pilot's license several years ago and for my birthday, invited me to fly with him. Since I had never flown with him, I jumped at the chance. Sure, I'd love to go!

On the designated morning, Duane and I met him at McCollum Airport in Kennesaw. Duane came along as the official photographer and observer. Robert went through the pre-flight ground inspection for the Cessna 172. It was a cute little white airplane. I had flown in commercial planes but never in a really small plane. Once the pre-flight inspection was finished, Robert said we were ready to board the plane.

One giant step and I was nestled inside the cozy little plane. Is that duct tape securing the window in the door? Now, I know duct tape when I see it and that was definitely duct tape! OK, Robert, why is duct tape on the door? He laughed and replied very calmly that the plane was an old plane and sometimes duct tape was needed. Then he assured me there was nothing to worry about. Alright, if he was sure.

He completed the internal inspections, then reached for the laminated "checklist chart". As I said, I'd never flown with Robert but he had been piloting for several years. Why did he need a checklist to tell him what to do? Not to worry, he assured me it was just being prudent and not taking any chances. Then he told me the story of a couple of pilots who had been flying many years and said they didn't need the checklist. Guess what? They headed out into the wild blue yonder without going through the checklist, crashed the plane and both pilots ended their careers (and lives) right then and there! That was certainly comforting information.

OK, checklist completed, instruments turned on. There were lots of dials and instruments in front of me. However, front and center was the flashing dial – LOW FUEL!!! Now, I'm not a pilot but I do know that it is not a good idea to fly when the fuel is low. Once again, I turned to Robert and trying to appear casual and relaxed (which I was not) inquired if we needed to make a stop for fuel. "Oh no, that gauge doesn't work. We have fuel." Really??? Then why is it flashing LOW FUEL? Again, Robert attempted to assure me that he had manually checked the fuel and that we did have fuel. Then he proceeded to explain that there were two fuel tanks and even if one ran out of fuel, we could fly with the other. Was that supposed to make me feel better? Alright, I really did have confidence in my son's flying ability but it sure would have been nicer without the duct tape and the LOW FUEL warning light!

Lift-off. Up we go! The runway was a little rough but once the wheels were off the ground, all was good. Wow! The scenery was beautiful – lots of trees. The lake and Allatoona Dam were serene from 3000 feet in the air.

Next, we flew over daughter, Allison's neighborhood. As Robert was explaining which house was Allison's he tilted the plane to one side so I could see better. Not a good idea as I grabbed for Robert's knee. OK, so he quickly ascertained that perhaps Mom was a little nervous leaning on her side attempting to find Allison's house. Quickly he leveled the plane and all was well again.

We flew over the Paulding County airport then back to McCollum Airport where Duane was waiting with camera in hand. Robert made a very smooth landing, the duct tape held the window in and we didn't run out of fuel. What more could I have asked for? It was a great (and certainly memorable) birthday!

WINDOW WITH A VIEW

There it was - twinkling like tiny diamonds in the night was the bridge over the Mississippi River at Natchez. As we gazed out our hotel window, the view was breathtaking! How many times have you heard the request for, "a room with a view?"   What an ethereal experience to look upon breath taking beauty so surreal it seems of another world. Although when we request, "a room with a view", we are usually referring to a gorgeous, magnificent ultra-beautiful view. However, there are times in our lives when we get something entirely different...

For instance, there was that special anniversary trip to Savannah. When I made the reservations, I specifically told the young man that I wanted a very nice room with a view. Now, that trip was in the middle of June of probably the hottest summer on record. After traveling ten long hours through a horrendous rain storm, we finally arrived at our destination.

When we were shown to our luxurious suite, the heat was so stifling, we could hardly breathe. Was there a problem with the air conditioning? The young man said that it wasn't working too well. That was an understatement! He said he'd turn the thermostat down and soon our little home away from home would be cool as could be. He left and we continued to perspire.

Trying to be as positive as possible, I walked over to the large windows in the living room and opened the long brown drapes. Oh no!!! Our "view" consisted of a narrow alley lined with trash cans and a dumpster. The brown draperies were quickly reclosed to cover the window. I called the manager and inquired about our supposedly beautiful view from the window. "Well, he drawled, it's like this..." Seems they put someone else in our beautiful room with a view because the air conditioning was not working in their room. Guess what room we were in? Yep, they put us in the room they had vacated. Did they think the air conditioning would magically start working???

We waited an hour for the room to cool but all to no avail. Thermostat was still reading 94 degrees so I called the manager. He said he'd send a maintenance person. About an hour later, the scruffy maintenance man arrived. When asked about the air conditioning, he replied, "Yep, ain't never going to cool this room – a cat got stuck in the pipes and he never came out. Ye can probably smell him later tonight." Well, that settled it! We packed our things and quickly checked out. Not exactly the anniversary we had planned, but life goes on.

Fast forward a few years. Hubby, Duane and I arrived at our hotel nestled in the quaint little town of Fair Hope, Alabama. We had been looking forward to this trip for several weeks. Since Duane and I are both writers, we knew we would enjoy Fair Hope which was home to many writers, poets and artists.

We checked into our hotel located in the middle of downtown. It was beautiful. Once in our room, we rushed to draw back the curtains covering a large picture window. Surely, we would see the glassy waters of Mobile Bay or the sandy white beaches. WRONG!!!

What we saw only about 5 feet from our window was a large rusty orange concrete wall. Surely there must be some vestige of scenic beauty somewhere. We moved closer to the window. We leaned first one way, then another. Shading the sun with our hand, we squinted our eyes. Surely, something was to be seen. We stood on tiptoe. Nothing. We stooped down lower until our knees bumped the lower wall. Nothing. Then trying one last time, we moved to the edge of the window, shaded the sun from our eyes, leaned over as far as we could without falling over, craned our necks and VOILA - We saw the tiniest tidbit of water. By that time, hysteria had set in. We were both laughing so hard, standing was almost impossible. So perhaps the view itself was not so much to be cherished, but the fun we had looking for it was a forever memory!
Room with a view after all!

REALLY IMPORTANT THINGS

A philosophy professor stood before his class and had some items in front of him. When class began, wordlessly he picked up a large empty mayonnaise jar and proceeded to fill it with rocks right to the top, rocks about two inches in diameter. He then asked the students if the jar was full. They agreed that it was.

So, the professor then picked up a box of pebbles and poured them into the jar. He shook the jar lightly. The pebbles, of course, rolled into the open areas between the rocks. The students laughed. He asked his students again if the jar was full. They agreed that yes, it was.

The professor then picked up a box of sand and poured it into the jar Of course, the sand filled up everything else. "Now", said the professor, "I want you to recognize that this is your life."

The rocks are the important things – your family, your partner, your health, your children – anything that is so important to you that if it were lost, you would be nearly destroyed. The pebbles are the other things in life that matter, but on a smaller scale. The pebbles represent things like your job, your house, your car. The sand is everything else, the small stuff.

If you put the sand or the pebbles into the jar first, there is not room for the rocks. The same goes for your life. If you spend all your energy and time on the small stuff, materials things, you will never have room for the things that are truly most important. Pay attention to the things that are critical in your life.

There will always be time to go to work, clean the house, give a dinner party and fix the disposal. Take care of the rocks first – the things that really matter. Set your priorities. The rest is just pebbles and sand.
Author Unknown

....

The really important things in our lives are not, "things" at all. They are interactions, relationships, opportunities to touch another's life in a positive way.

Many of us have felt God's nudging to do something good in everyday circumstances: volunteer in a local soup kitchen, offer to carry someone's groceries, allow someone to go in front of you at the checkout line, donate items to charitable organizations and on and on. But being the recipient of some kindnesses is often unexpected and leaves us pondering what our response should be.

One day, Duane and I were eating breakfast in our local Waffle House. We went there often and knew most of the servers by name. As we were getting ready to leave, Duane asked for the check. Our server said we didn't have a check, that the nicely dressed African American lady who had been sitting at the counter had paid our bill. We were totally shocked.

Although over the years, we had paid for many other people's meals, neither of us had ever had someone pay for our meal. We had seen the lady sitting there but we didn't know her. She had not spoken to us nor we her. Did this lady think we were destitute and unable to pay for our meal? We didn't think so. We were dressed reasonably well and doubted there was anything about us that indicated poverty – but why had she paid for our meal?

We never knew the answer to our question and we never saw the well-dressed lady again but her action remained in our memory and hearts. We'll probably never know how she chose us for her generosity, but it continues to motivate us to be aware of others and to always reach out whenever opportunity presents itself.

I'd like to share another experience that has grown exponentially in a most unexpected way for me. As a recent cancer survivor, I was blessed to encounter many very inspirational women along the way. Here is my story...

We sat nameless in the women's waiting room, each pondering our own situations. There was a young mother whose hair was beginning to grow back. She was always smiling – only 15 more treatments to go. In a wheelchair to my left sat a beautiful woman wearing a red shirt with golden sunflowers on it and a matching crocheted hat. Bright sunflower earrings framed her face. An older lady hugged me gently and said, "We are so lucky. God is with us and we are going to be alright."

The days became weeks and our journeys continued. I felt blessed to be in the presence of such inspiring and courageous women. I wanted to return their gifts of inspiration and encouragement, but I questioned what I had to give. My body was weak, my stamina drained. What could I give?

The answer came in the late hours of a sleepless night. I could write! I am a poet and a photographer. I wrote a collection of inspirational poems and incorporated my favorite photos. That was the birth of THE POETRY CARDS. Each set of POETRY CARDS contained thirteen different poems. The cards were neatly packaged in clear plastic. Included was my story of how they came to be. I also included my name, phone number and email address.

They were a small token of my appreciation for all the inspirational, courageous women I met on my challenging journey. It was my hope that the verses I wrote might touch someone's heart, bring a smile to their face or make their day a little brighter.

At first, I printed only twenty-five sets of THE POETRY CARDS and gave them to the ladies in the oncology waiting rooms. Then one day, I saw a lady in a wheel chair in the grocery store. She had a walking cane laying across her lap. The walking cane had been decorated with colorful stickers. Something just spoke to me and I knew I had to share the POETRY CARDS with my unknown friend. I walked over to her and introduced myself. I told her I would like to give her something and handed her the cards. As she read the story about the cards, she shared with me her situation. She was so grateful for the very small gift I had given her. She was such a blessing to me.

Another afternoon, Duane and I were driving down Hwy. 41 in Marietta. A young lady wearing a pink hat was in the median of the highway collecting money. Again, I felt God's nudging so while we were stopped at the traffic light, I reached out my car window, dropped a few dollars into her bucket and told her I would like to give her something. I handed her the POETRY CARDS and before I could say anything else, the traffic light turned green and we drove on down the highway. A couple of days later, I received an email from her telling me her story. She was collecting money for her participation in the Susan G. Komen Race for the Cure cancer walk. She had family members who were battling cancer. A few weeks later, I received a nice thank you note from the Susan G. Komen Foundation. Once again, the young lady in the pink hat was a blessing to me.

One evening, I received a phone call from a gentleman I had never met. He said he was at the post office that afternoon and as he was about to purchase some mailing materials, he spotted a set of my POETRY CARDS lying on the counter. He picked them up and told the postal worker, he would like to purchase them. Suddenly, a lady near him grabbed the cards from his hand and said they were not for sale, that they belonged to her. She said they were given to her. She allowed him to look at the cards and to get my phone number. He called me and asked if he could purchase a set of cards for his wife. She was dealing with some very serious health problems. I told him I did not sell the cards but I would be happy to give them to his wife. The cards were in the mail the following day and a few days later, his wife called me. We talked for almost an hour. Again, the blessing was mine.

Since I made the first pack of POETRY CARDS, I have printed over 250 sets, all of which I have given away. I make and package all the cards myself. They are never sold but are freely given to anyone who might want them. The blessings I have received have been unbelievable. It's amazing how God works through us even when we feel we have nothing to give!

So, as the philosophy professor so eloquently stated, *"Take care of the rocks first – the things that really matter. Set your priorities. The rest is just pebbles and sand."*

ABOUT THE AUTHOR

 Ann Lovvorn Douglass is a retired elementary principal. She holds an Educational Specialist Degree from the State University of West Georgia, Master of Education, and Bachelor of Science Degrees from Georgia State University. Prior to her retirement, she served as principal at Blackwell Elementary and Belmont Hills Elementary Schools in Cobb County, GA.

Published books (in the name of Ann R. Lovvorn) include: **PURPLE FROGS AND PUMPKIN SEEDS**, **CHOCOLATE PUDDLES** and **THE COOKIE BOOK**. She is a Distinguished Member of the International Poet Fellows and a member of the International Who's Who in Poetry. Other published works include: *An Angel in the Shelter*; *Patriotism, Peace and Love Through the Eyes of a Child;* and *The Little Boy's Hand.* Each of these was awarded the Editor's Choice Award for Outstanding Achievement in Poetry by the International Library of Poetry.

Ann Lovvorn Douglass lives in Kennesaw, GA with her husband, Duane. Between them, they have six children and nine grandchildren.

annrdouglass@outlook.com
120 Chastain Rd., NW   Unit 2107
Kennesaw, GA 30144
(770) 365-4409

Made in the USA
Columbia, SC
02 November 2017